The World Trade Organization

A Beginner's Guide

"Commendable, clear and thoughtful. This will make it much easier for the non-expert to understand the organization."

David A. Gantz, Samuel M. Fegtly Professor of Law and Co-Director, International Trade and Business Law Program, University of Arizona

"A concise and insightful introduction to the intricacies of a poorly understood institution. Using a jargon-free style and focusing on what matters most, this is an invaluable tool for anyone interested in learning what the WTO is about."

Dr Gabriel Gari, Senior Lecturer in International Economic Law, Centre for Commercial Law Studies, Queen Mary University of London

ONEWORLD BEGINNER'S GUIDES combine an original, inventive and engaging approach with expert analysis. Innovative and affordable, books in the series are perfect for anyone curious about the way the world works and the big ideas of our time.

aesthetics
africa
american politics
anarchism
animal behaviour
anthropology
anti-capitalism
aquinas
archaeology
art
artificial intelligence
the baha'i faith
the beat generation
the bible
biodiversity
bioterror & biowarfare
the brain
british politics
the Buddha
cancer
censorship
christianity
civil liberties
classical music
climate change
cloning
the cold war
conservation
crimes against humanity
criminal psychology
critical thinking
the crusades
daoism
democracy
descartes
dewey

dyslexia
energy
engineering
the english civil wars
the enlightenment
epistemology
ethics
the european union
evolution
evolutionary psychology
existentialism
fair trade
feminism
forensic science
french literature
the french revolution
genetics
global terrorism
hinduism
the history of medicine
history of science
homer
humanism
huxley
iran
islamic philosophy
the islamic veil
journalism
judaism
lacan
life in the universe
literary theory
machiavelli
mafia & organized crime
magic
marx

medieval philosophy
the middle east
modern slavery
NATO
the new testament
nietzsche
nineteenth-century art
the northern ireland conflict
nutrition
oil
opera
the palestine–israeli conflict
particle physics
paul
philosophy
philosophy of mind
philosophy of religion
philosophy of science
planet earth
postmodernism
psychology
quantum physics
the qur'an
racism
reductionism
religion
renaissance art
the roman empire
the russian revolution
shakespeare
the small arms trade
sufism
the torah
the united nations
volcanoes
world war II

The World Trade Organization

Organization

A Beginner's Guide

David Collins

ONEWORLD

A Oneworld Paperback Original

Published in North America, Great Britain and Australia by
Oneworld Publications, 2015

ISBN 978-1-78074-578-7
eISBN 978-1-74074-579-4

Typeset by Silicon Chips
Printed and bound in Great Britain
by Clays Ltd, St Ives plc

Oneworld Publications
10 Bloomsbury Street
London WC1B 3SR
England

Contents

List of acronyms

ASEAN:	Association of Southeast Asian Nations
BIT:	Bilateral Investment Treaty
EPA:	Economic Partnership Agreement
FDI:	Foreign Direct Investment
GATS:	General Agreement on Trade in Services
GATT:	General Agreement on Tariffs and Trade
GDP:	Gross Domestic Product
GSP:	Generalized System of Preferences
GMO:	Genetically Modified Organism
IMF:	International Monetary Fund
MERCOSUR:	Southern Common Market
NAFTA:	North American Free Trade Agreement
NGO:	Non-Governmental Organization
RTA:	Regional Trade Agreement
SCM:	Agreement on Subsidies and Countervailing Measures
SPS:	Agreement on Sanitary and Phytosanitary Measures
TBT:	Agreement on Technical Barriers to Trade
TRIPS:	Agreement on Trade-Related Aspects of Intellectual Property
UN:	United Nations
WTO:	World Trade Organization

Introduction

The World Trade Organization (WTO) is one of the most important and controversial organizations in the world. While it has helped bring millions of people out of poverty and raised standards of living worldwide, it strikes at the heart of what it means for a country to be independent and control its own destiny. As a lynchpin of globalization, the WTO allows us to enjoy products and services from around the world, but it lays bare the frailty of many industries, in some cases causing unemployment and even threatening social cohesion. Whether it should be seen as an agent of good or evil may depend on where you live and what you do, much as it does on what you buy and where it comes from.

How does the WTO function as a global organization which creates and enforces the rules of international trade between countries? What are the principal goals that the WTO seeks to achieve, and how have these created difficulties for its member countries as they adapt to the pressures of globalization? In this book, I will tackle these questions while focusing on the main legal obligations of WTO membership. I will also consider the economic justification for its rules and the ways in which these are balanced against national policy goals, such as economic self-sufficiency, environmental protection and cultural preservation. Even at twenty years old, the continued relevance of the WTO is under threat. This is possibly because of its over-enlarged mandate, the difficulties in ongoing negotiations for deeper trade liberalization among its 161 member countries and, perhaps most importantly, because of the growth of bilateral trade agreements like the Transatlantic Trade and Investment Partnership and the

Trans-Pacific Partnership. Still, it remains a vital instrument of governance in the global economy.

Too often, discussion of the WTO descends into controversy surrounding the WTO's alleged detrimental impact on the global economy, especially on poor countries. While some of these accusations have grains of truth in them – certainly some farmers in Africa would be able to sell more food if there were no agricultural subsidies in Europe – I hope that my treatment of the rules and principles that underlie the WTO will allow you to form your own view of the organization and the merits of international trade. In that sense, this book will be neither a ponderous textbook nor a provocative rant against globalization. It will also not shy away from the harsh reality that, largely because of the WTO, many factory workers in the West have seen their jobs shipped overseas, while at the same time consumers like you and me have been able to get more bang for their buck on everyday things like clothes and electronics.

The WTO embraces the philosophy that free trade, or more accurately freer trade, is the route to economic progress. The opening paragraph of the treaty which established the WTO states that the purpose of the WTO is to raise standards of living worldwide, ensure full employment and a large and steadily growing volume of real income while allowing for the optimal use of the world's resources. So, right from the outset, the WTO concedes that its goal is not free trade at all costs. Free trade is merely an instrument to achieve more important objectives, namely living well and with self-sufficiency. These are aims which themselves must be balanced against the need to safeguard the natural environment by avoiding depletion of the raw materials upon which this prosperity depends. The WTO treaty goes on to state that the benefits of trade should be shared by all countries, not only the rich ones, a clear recognition that unbridled competition can have harmful consequences for the unprepared and inexperienced. This qualification is particularly important because more than two thirds of the WTO member countries are classified as developing. The extent to which the WTO has succeeded in achieving these goals is a matter of debate as well as the subject of empirical analysis.

Although the WTO itself is only twenty years old, international trade has been around for many centuries. The founders of the WTO cannot take credit for inventing it, or even for being the first to recognize its value. Economic historians often cite the Phoenicians as the first international traders, plying the waters of the eastern Mediterranean Sea on sailing ships from about 1500 BCE to exchange things like dyes and wood with settlements throughout the region. Centuries later the Silk Road was established as a land trading route between eastern Europe (then controlled by the Roman Empire) through the civilizations of Middle East all the way out to the Pacific Ocean. This crucial conduit through the mountains and deserts of central Asia allowed the trading of commodities like spice and silk, making a significant contribution to the economic development of civilizations like Persia, China and Europe itself. By the end of the Middle Ages, seafaring had become the dominant means of international trade, with ships from western European kingdoms setting out across the world's oceans to bring cargo's of precious metals and commodities like tea to ports in London and Amsterdam from Africa and the Far East, just as Western merchants introduced new crops and animals to China, Japan and the East Indies.

In a cycle that calls to mind the ups and downs of our modern economies, international trade went into decline, at least in the West, during the mercantilist era of the fifteenth to eighteenth centuries. Mercantilism was an economic theory practised by many European nations that promoted heavy restrictions on imports coupled with the accumulation of monetary reserves. During this period exports of gold and silver were prohibited, colonies were forbidden to trade with one another and trade on foreign ships was outlawed. These restrictions on the free flow of goods around the world are associated with a period of economic stagnation and are now widely viewed as a misguided attempt to ensure the self-sufficiency of the nation state in times of crisis. But by cutting themselves off from cheaper sources of various goods around the world, Western nations doomed themselves to more labour with ultimately less consumption. It was isolation, not trade, that was the source of their demise.

To understand why, historically, international trade is associated with prosperity and the advancement of civilization, whereas impediments to trade are linked to the reverse, we can look to the theory of 'comparative advantage', developed by the British economist David Ricardo in the early nineteenth century. This idea is the economic and logical justification for why trade among nations should be as free as possible. In that sense it is the ideological foundation of the WTO.

The Nobel Prize-winning economist Paul Samuelson was once challenged to name one proposition in all of the social sciences which is both true and non-trivial (not obvious) – Samuelson responded with comparative advantage. The theory (echoing ideas that had been expressed by Adam Smith in *The Wealth of Nations* some decades earlier) states that nations should specialize in the production of that which they are relatively best at and trade to obtain everything else. In Ricardo's famous example, if Portugal is better both at making shirts and making wine than England, but it is better at making wine than it is at making shirts, it should spend all of its labour making wine and let England spend all its labour making shirts. A greater total wealth of shirts and wine will be produced with this specialization, and the two countries can trade for each other's wine and shirts. This logic holds true even for countries that aren't the best at anything (as England in the example); they should still focus on making what they are least bad at. In this way countries capture efficiencies, extract more value from each unit of energy (hour of labour) spent in producing a particular good and still enjoy a whole suite of products by obtaining other more efficiently produced items from other places.

But comparative advantage only works when international trade is free – meaning that it is not frustrated by barriers in the form of restrictive laws, like high customs duties or import bans. Protectionism, which was practised widely from the mercantilist period until the mid-twentieth century, consisted of precisely that – protecting closed markets by erecting legal obstacles to free trade. Not only did this cause goods from abroad to become more expensive, it arguably contributed to the two World Wars, because countries were not economically dependent upon one another, allowing natural rivalries to fester. Trade isolationism left countries disinterested in the prosperity of their neighbours, drawn instead to the idea that any advancement must necessarily be at the expense of someone else's decline. Many agree that this attitude was responsible for the Great Depression of the 1930s, because it created scarcities in essential goods obtained from abroad. During the Communist era many people in the USSR never tasted 'exotic' foods like bananas or oranges, let alone luxury treats like chocolate. Ordinary consumer goods like jeans were widely coveted in countries like the former Yugoslavia.

The classic form of protectionism has until recent times been the tariff, essentially a fee placed on all incoming foreign goods to render them artificially more expensive so that domestic goods appear cheaper to consumers, eliminating the demand for imports. This is helpful to inefficient domestic suppliers, but bad for consumers who end up paying more. Even worse, outright bans or quotas (limits on the volume of goods from abroad) make foreign goods not just more expensive, but often impossible to obtain. This not only restricts options available to us, the people who buy things, but can even lead to shortages of goods and soaring prices. Drought in Russia in 2010 resulted in Moscow imposing a (legal) wheat export ban, which ultimately wreaked havoc in international grain markets, to the delight of some traders as well as farmers in Canada. Of course, it was not well received by the people who eat cereal every day.

Modern forms of trade protectionism include things like subsidization (effectively governmental assistance for its own producers) and excessive technical regulation in the guise of health and safety precautions. It is not clear that Ricardo's original justification for free trade based on the theory of comparative advantage speaks directly to these concerns, many of which are tied closely to varying approaches to domestic governance rather than issues of international trade. What might seem a trade-distortive subsidy to an economist may be seen as within the sphere of governmental supervision to politicians from many parts of the world. Similarly, health and safety regulations may appear as 'nanny state' interference to one person, but fulfilling a legitimate custodial duty to another.

We now know that there is a clear statistical link between freer trade and economic growth. Liberal trade policies which allow for the unrestricted flow of goods and services facilitate competition, which in turn stimulates innovation, generating both wealth and employment. Adapting to competition, either nationally or from outside one's own borders, can be difficult, often leading to factory shutdowns and lay-offs on a large scale, especially in the short term. The opportunity for manufacturing in developing countries has worsened job losses in places where wages were high (or too high, as many economists would argue), like the US Midwest and the North of England. Mass unemployment and economic stagnation ensued because workforces could not withstand competition from labourers grateful to escape a life of subsistence farming. The empty shell of the city of Detroit, once the focal point of the American car-manufacturing miracle, is perhaps the most extreme example of globalization's scourge. It is a symbol of the painful incapacity of firms, governments and ordinary people to adapt to change, no matter how much fore-warning they are given.

Despite the benefits of cheaper and more diverse products, there is undeniably a mood of fear and helplessness associated with the presence of foreign goods on our shelves, even if we end up buying them because they are so cheap. Anxiety about the rise of China and the loss of competitiveness of the West is a common theme in the modern media. Dambisa Moyo's bestselling book *How the West was Lost* chronicles the failed economic policies of Europe and the US that led to their apparent 'decline' relative to Asian countries. Naomi Klein's groundbreaking book, *No Logo*, which depicts the devastating effect of consumerism and corporatism on worldwide poverty, is probably still regarded as the bible of the anti-globalization movement. These books capture the angst of liberal intellectuals who struggle with the reality that the workings of international markets often mean that some people will lose out.

Unfortunately, many of the proponents of anti-globalization, glamorized recently by the urban tents of the worldwide Occupy movement, fail to appreciate that the WTO (perhaps the classic embodiment of globalization in one institution) is not controlled by self-serving, power-hungry political and corporate elites. It is a democratically constituted body that is governed by and subject to the rule of law. By this I mean that while it creates rules about free trade, it, meaning its member countries, is also bound by them. No one nation and certainly no one person or corporation is above the legal obligations imposed by the WTO. To the extent that the WTO permits its rules to be broken, there are conditions placed on when and how this can happen, many of which entail unpleasant, although sometimes necessary consequences. Still, the rules of the WTO are themselves often uneven. Just as subsidies on manufactured goods are generally prohibited, those linked to agriculture are largely undisciplined – a clear bias in favour of industrialized states which are strong in manufacturing but weak in farming.

The importance of law to the understanding of how the WTO functions is the main theme of this book. It is impossible to appreciate the way in which the WTO works and to form a critical opinion about it without coming to terms with the legal obligations at its core. So, instead of taking you on a journey through the historical and political origins of how the WTO came to be in the aftermath of World War II at the pivotal economic conference of the Allied Powers in Bretton Woods, New Hampshire, in 1944 (because these events, while important, say very little about how and why the WTO does the things that it does today), I will instead paint a picture of the main legal principles within the WTO. These laws constitute both the edifice on which global trade is founded and (to mix metaphors) the breeze that clears out the cobwebs of protectionism and red tape, freeing up business to promote economic progress around the world.

1
How it works: the structure and function of the WTO

A few years ago, while flipping through one of the WTO's own publications aimed at informing the general public about what it does, I was struck by a comment near the beginning that said the WTO is best described as a table. This statement wasn't meant to evoke a metaphysical or Freudian discussion. It was simply intended to capture the fact that the WTO is focused on allowing people to talk about things so that they can eventually come to an agreement, just as people sit around tables to negotiate. The table itself does nothing.

The WTO on its own has no interests or agenda apart from that of its constituent members. It is entirely member-driven and in that sense it is democratic, which does not fit the image of an old boys' club of big business special interest that is often perpetuated by the media. Of course, no state would tolerate its trade policy being dictated to solely by any particular commercial interest. This is why it's not fair to say that the WTO should do this or it should do that. 'It' can only do what its members want, which is itself up to the will of elected politicians around the world.

The organization

The WTO came into being on 1 January 1995 as a result of many years of negotiation among the signatory states of a treaty called the General Agreement on Tariffs and Trade (GATT), which is an international agreement among individual countries promoting free international trade in goods. In its simplest form, the WTO's objective is to administer the GATT as well as a series of other international agreements on trade, many of which will be explored throughout this book. The WTO is headquartered in Geneva, Switzerland.

The will of the WTO is exercised through its members, and the WTO's membership is currently composed of 161 countries at the time of writing in mid-2015. Members must be countries and only countries – not companies, cities or non-governmental organizations (NGOs). The European Union (EU), which is a member of the WTO, is strictly speaking a supranational collection of countries, but they act in unison for the purposes of international trade. With the accession of Russia in 2012, WTO membership now includes all of the major trading countries in the world. In fact, the only countries that are outside the system are those that have largely isolated themselves from world affairs, such as North Korea. In that sense, almost the entire world's seven billion people fall under the influence of the WTO in some way.

The process for joining the WTO, known formally as accession, is different for each new member country. Each member negotiates an individually tailored agreement – called an Accession Protocol, setting out the precise terms under which it agrees to join the WTO community. This must be approved by every existing member. Common conditions attached to new members include phase-in periods for countries that are not yet full market economies, which may involve the gradual opening up of various sectors or industries to international trade over time rather than suddenly. Accession negotiations can often take many years, a fact which reflects both the difficulties involved for some countries bringing their economies into line with the WTO's principles as well as how important WTO membership has become. In many ways WTO membership is a badge of integration into the world economy – a statement that a country is mature enough to interact in economic affairs on the world stage.

Each member has equal standing at the WTO, meaning that in theory each one has the same capacity to effect change through voting. The one-nation-one-vote ideology suggests that in one sense the WTO is truly democratic, unlike some other international organizations, like the International Monetary Fund (IMF), where voting power is allocated according to the size of each country's economy. Of course in reality the larger, more powerful members like the US and the EU exercise greater decision-making influence because they are able to offer more concessions as bargaining chips, allowing greater access to their large lucrative markets in exchange for voting allegiance. As with most international organizations, there is a significant democratic deficit in the governance of the WTO. Strategic voting through alliance formation is most commonly associated these days with developing states that tend to negotiate at the WTO in blocs. Allegiances of this kind have had limited impact in the past because of the often superficial nature of shared interests among developing countries, which tends to break down under tight negotiations. Also, some of the larger developing countries that were expected to take on leadership roles at the WTO, such as India and China, failed to do so, often pursuing their own interests at the expense of other developing country members. India's recent holdout over its food security programme, which did not fit with the WTO's subsidy rules, is a good example of this.

One of the major criticisms of the WTO was that the real negotiations take place in smaller groups, with many of the least powerful member countries effectively marginalized from the true power-brokering. Informal discussions known as 'Green Room' meetings (so-called because of the colour of the walls of the Director-General's conference room in which they took place) were unrepresentative and non-inclusive. The results of these critical meetings among the most important players were then brought to the formally democratic process of full WTO membership for voting, but little practical input was possible by that point. This system of privileged debate led to accusations that the WTO was insufficiently transparent, with the vast majority of the membership (the weak developing countries) having little to no practical say in the organization's management. Green Room-type meetings have largely been eliminated in recent years, with the Director-General reporting back to all members the results of any informal gatherings held in his offices.

Each of the WTO's members agrees to abide by its various agreements, including the original GATT from the 1940s and a host of new agreements that were established in 1995 along with the creation of the WTO itself. They are legally binding obligations that compel the member countries to ensure that their laws relating to trade are kept within limits that have been set by the WTO community. We will be looking at many of the most important of these agreements throughout this book. In so doing, we will also see how the WTO resolves disputes that arise between the members about what exactly these agreements require them to do, and what happens if they are not followed. It is important to recognize that WTO rules do not bind people or companies, at least not directly. They apply only to the member countries, which in turn create laws that affect private citizens and firms.

Negotiations among the WTO members are an ongoing process, but it is organized into sessions that are known as 'rounds'. Each negotiating round can last several years. Since the creation of the GATT in the late 1940s, there have been eight rounds of trade negotiations. The eighth one, the Uruguay Round, named after the location of where it was commenced, ran from 1986 to 1994 and resulted in the creation of the WTO itself. A ninth round, the Doha Round, began in 2001 and is still under way.

This doesn't mean that the negotiations still take place in Doha – this is simply where they began. The Doha Round is aimed at ensuring that the economic globalization brought about by the WTO is made more inclusive, helping the world's poorest people, in particular by cutting subsidies to agriculture, such as those instigated by the US and the EU. As we will see later on, so far, work towards achieving this objective has met with limited success.

The initial purpose of the negotiations, which began under GATT in the 1940s, was to lower tariffs or customs duties on foreign goods, but by the mid-1990s tariffs had become so low, barely four percent on average, that the negotiations switched focus to other barriers to internationally traded goods, like subsidies and rules on health and safety. Negotiations also expanded from goods to things like services and intellectual property.

In addition to the ongoing negotiation rounds, there are regular meetings of the Ministerial Conference, which is the highest decision-making body of the WTO, composed of representatives of each of its members. There have been nine Ministerial Conferences since the WTO was established, roughly one every two years. The first one was held over a few days in Singapore in 1996, with the conference in Bali in December 2013 the most recent. The third conference, held in Seattle in 1999, resulted in mass demonstrations by various groups including anti-globalizationists, environmentalists and labour unions, as well as anarchists opposing all forms of government. Photos and video clips of the Seattle demonstrations, some of which were quite violent, are still among the most evocative impressions many people have of the WTO. In many respects the Seattle Ministerial Conference was the first time the eyes of the world's media were focused on the then four-year-old organization. Some feel that the swift response of the US National Guard in controlling the protests permanently tarnished the image of the WTO as a democratic and open institution.

As much of the WTO's work is highly specialized, there are a number of committees and agencies within it that are tasked with certain duties. For example, the Trade Policy Review mechanism is a special team of experts that engages in periodic evaluations of the status of each member's international trade laws. Reports are produced by this body effectively summarizing the extent to which each country is complying with its WTO laws. This data acts as a useful form of advice to traders on the types of barriers they are likely to encounter when exporting to a given member country. While each member of the WTO is reviewed through this system, the frequency of review depends on the economic size of the country, with the larger members being reviewed more often. The Trade Policy Review system is a key component of the WTO's mission (on behalf of its members, of course) to share information about international trade laws, which itself is seen as a vital instrument of trade liberalization.

Another important agency within the WTO is the Committee on Regional Trade Agreements. This group considers whether regional trade agreements among some but not all of the WTO's members fit within its global rules. Regional agreements must be notified to this committee, which then evaluates their legitimacy from a perspective of the WTO's overall rules, and importantly publishes them in a database of regional agreements available to all WTO members. More than 580 such agreements have been notified to this committee as of late 2014.

Perhaps the most distinct branch of the WTO is its Dispute Settlement Body. The Dispute Settlement Body is a special arm of the WTO that resolves disputes between WTO members about the meaning and implementation of the organization's various rules on international trade. The activities of the Dispute Settlement Body in allowing the smooth administration of the various WTO agreements will be explored more closely in chapter 3.

With all these activities (group voting, rule-making, information dissemination and dispute settlement) it is no surprise that the WTO incurs some considerable operational costs. The total budget for the WTO is around US $200 million per year, which is small given the relative importance of the organization to the global economy. It has a permanent staff of about 640 people, most of whom are engaged in administrative support. This is less, for example, than the budget and staff of the IMF or the World Bank, let alone an agency of the size of the United Nations. In the interests of transparency, each year the WTO issues its Annual Report, which outlines its activities and provides a detailed breakdown of information about its budget and staffing.

THE WTO DIRECTOR-GENERAL

The top official in the WTO is the Director-General. This person is the chief representative of the organization itself, responsible for issuing policy statements about the WTO's activities and its take on current issues in international economic affairs as well as the more routine duty of supervising the WTO's internal administrative functions. Because the work of the WTO can be highly political, involving the cooperation of many hundreds of diplomats and their governments, the position is well suited to an individual who has a political or policy background, rather than someone from the private sector or industry, who may be more accustomed to giving orders that go unchallenged. Past Directors-General have included Mike Moore, a former prime minister of New Zealand; Pascal Lamy, former president of the European Commission; and Peter Sutherland, the former attorney general of Ireland. As of 2014, there has yet to be a female Director-General of the WTO. The current Director-General is Robert Azevêdo, who took office in September 2013. He is a former diplomat from Brazil and the first Latin American to hold the top post of the organization. Azevêdo had long-term involvement with the WTO, acting on behalf of Brazil in a number of disputes as well as sitting as a judge in several dispute settlement cases. His participation in the WTO judicial procedures is curious given that he trained as an engineer, although this seeming inconsistency illustrates how the WTO's rules are implemented in a highly pragmatic fashion, even while they are on occasion also legally technical. After laborious and often tense negotiations, Azevêdo earned early praise in December 2013 for his vital role in cementing the important Bali agreements on food security and cutting trade bureaucracy. He emerged as something of an eleventh-hour hero in the media's depiction of the marathon discussions, where he insisted that failure to reach accord was not an option. While it is unlikely that the WTO will ever enjoy the representation of someone quite as appealing as Angelina Jolie (as ambassador for the United Nations High Commissioner for Refugees), Roberto Azevêdo may be as good as the WTO can expect in the way of a figurehead for the time being.

The WTO headquarters are in the Centre William Rappard on Geneva's Rue de Lausanne. The complex, originally constructed in the 1920s, is set among trees in a park next to Lake Geneva, about a twenty-minute walk from the centre of the city; much of the building's artwork – depicting people at various forms of work – is a reminder that it was originally the home of the International Labour Office. An extension to the old, mostly stone and brick building was completed in 2013. The extension includes an underground car park as well as new office space and several additional meeting rooms. Overall, the complex has a pleasing mix of old-world gravitas (echoing hallways with high, ornate ceilings and huge doors) and modern (glass and steel). It also boasts low energy consumption, with solar panels for water heating and sophisticated insulation. Not bad for 200 million dollars.

Still, the fact that the WTO headquarters are effectively hidden behind the cover of trees and an imposing wall in the mountains of Switzerland does not help the organization's image as a transparent, accessible and democratic global institution. It looks more like a James Bond villain's lair than a public building. Although the WTO is geographically remote and physically impenetrable (good luck getting inside the Centre William

Rappard without a written invitation from someone important!), it has always been well ahead of the game in terms of its public outreach through the Internet. The WTO website is remarkably complete, up to date and user-friendly. And while the same could now be said of the websites of a number of international institutions, like the World Bank or the IMF, the WTO's website has always been accessible, even during the early days of the Internet.

The WTO's mandate

The essential objective of the WTO is to minimize obstacles to global trade. While its mandate has expanded from its mid-twentieth-century focus on trade in manufactured goods to capture the movement of intangibles like services as well as intellectual property, and its efforts have shifted away from tariffs to other forms of protectionism like subsidies, the WTO has remained true to its original ideal. It is a trade organization, so to the extent that its activities touch on other policy areas, it only deals with them in as much as they affect trade. The WTO is careful to restrict its involvement to only those matters which are truly trade related. This narrow focus has attracted criticism, primarily because failure to deal with other related and often vital issues of global concern could be seen as a wasted opportunity or short-sightedness. Since the WTO has considerable credibility in terms of its engagement with the global community, it is well placed to weigh in on various pressing policy matters. But it has generally chosen not to.

There are several key issues that remain beyond the scope of the WTO. First, it has no formal competency over matters relating directly to labour, including either the wages of employees or their working conditions around the world. Of course, any time a trade rule affects someone's ability to obtain and keep their job, then labour issues are clearly engaged. This tension has been the source of considerable criticism because of the obvious link between efficiency in the production and export of goods (especially manufactured ones) and low wages. In theory, firms gain a competitive advantage by paying their workers less – their goods become cheaper in world markets than those produced by firms whose employees are paid relatively more. This strategy has itself been called into question. Paying workers higher wages often leads to more productive output, but the fact remains that labour-intensive companies tend to locate where wages are low (currently East Asia, especially Vietnam and Thailand, now that wages in China have begun to rise). While WTO supporters could quite rightly assert that wages are the responsibility of domestic governments and not an aspect of international trade law or policy, this argument loses some credibility because employees have little to no bargaining power vis-à-vis their employers because, unlike companies, they are not internationally mobile. Workers cannot readily move to where there are jobs or where wages are higher because of strictly enforced immigration laws around the world. Indeed, it is often said that while the WTO has established global markets for goods and services, it has done nothing to achieve the final pillar of globalization – the free movement of people across borders.

Much to the consternation of the Green movement and NGOs like Friends of the Earth and Greenpeace, in one sense the WTO doesn't have anything to do with the environment or climate change either, at least not directly. Members of the WTO are not required to make any commitments not to pollute the air or water or to preserve wildlife. That's up to the governments of each of the member countries. In another very real sense, an issue that may seem to be trade related may to another person be viewed as an environmental matter. The WTO does allow members to have their own policies on protecting the environment, even where this might have an adverse effect on international trade. The WTO tries not to get in the way of environmental protection, even though it doesn't proactively aim to do anything to save the natural world as part of its formal mandate. It could do more – but then it would cease being an organization devoted to liberalizing international trade and would become something quite different, more like a system of global government.

It is worth pointing out that the international trade of goods is not as damaging to the environment as some critics may believe. The carbon footprint of products sourced from across the world, like exotic fruits, is not necessarily higher than those which are produced locally. This is because there are many factors that influence the carbon emissions associated with a given item, only one of which relates to transportation. For example, maintaining greenhouses in colder climates is itself carbon intensive, as are many mechanized production techniques. Contrary to what you might think, a 2007 study by Cranfield University in the UK showed that flowers imported into the UK from Kenya are less environmentally damaging than those imported across the Channel from the Netherlands!

Perhaps somewhat closer to home in terms of economic policies, the WTO also has no control over tax issues, at least not directly. It does not dictate to its members how they should collect personal or corporate income tax. But if some types of taxes act as barriers to trade – such as sales tax on foreign goods, or excise taxes that act as barriers to entry of foreign products, then the WTO is quite happy to get involved. Taxes are one way that governments can engage in discrimination against foreign goods, making them appear more expensive and therefore unattractive to consumers. This is precisely the type of distortive behaviour that the WTO seeks to prevent.

CURRENCY WARS

A country can make its exports artificially more attractive (cheaper) than those from other countries by lowering the exchange value of its currency. With a weak relative currency, more products which that country produces can be bought for less. This is an unfair advantage that skews international trade in favour of countries with weaker currencies. Manipulating currency value is so effective that it can actually undo all of the progress achieved through GATT and the WTO in terms of tariff reductions – a country can replace the rents imposed through illegal tariffs by lowering the value of its money. This is one reason why currency manipulation is prohibited by the IMF. But the IMF has very little power to police this rule, and this is why a number of countries continue to engage in this practice, dubbed 'Currency Wars' by the Brazilian economist who first drew attention to the fact that a number of countries were competitively devaluing their own currencies against one another in order to deal with the global financial crisis. It is very difficult to prove that this is actually taking place, especially since some of the tools used to weaken currencies have legitimate economic objectives, such as quantitative easing – the notorious practice of printing more money to help deal with indebtedness. China was accused by the US and other countries of artificially devaluing the renminbi to boost its exports, allowing its cheap goods to flood world markets. China shot back that the US was effectively doing the same thing with its quantitative easing programme. Many economists accordingly have called upon the WTO to take steps to prevent currency wars. While the WTO has no direct competency over monetary relations, it does aim to prevent protectionism, which competitive valuation clearly is. Unfortunately there is nothing in the GATT or any of the WTO treaties that specifically prevents WTO members from engaging in currency manipulation, other than the rather vague statement in the GATT that countries should fulfil their IMF obligations and that the WTO itself should cooperate with the IMF. This gap is viewed as a major hole in the WTO's rules that has the potential to unravel completely the organization's entire anti-protectionist framework.

Another sphere of economic or commercial activity that falls outside the WTO's domain is competition law, or antitrust law as it is known in the US and Canada. This is perhaps the most glaring omission in terms of the WTO's role. Surely the ability of markets to function free from monopolies or otherwise dominant influences is a necessary feature of properly functioning competitive markets. But a key point to remember about the WTO is that its objectives are international, not national. The WTO is concerned about the normal functioning of global markets, not national ones. So the WTO leaves it up to each member country to enact competition or antitrust laws in order to ensure that damaging monopolistic practices like price controls are not employed by firms. Similarly, when multinational companies demonstrate harmful market dominance, they should be controlled by the national laws of the countries in which they operate. This is because the WTO's concern is not with corporate structure – how big or powerful a company has become – but simply whether any good (regardless of which firm produces it) is able to enter foreign markets freely. There may come a time when a global competition law is established – many commentators have urged greater international coordination in this sphere – but for now it is left up to national governments on their own. However, if a national law aimed at regulating competition were to have an adverse effect on international trade, the WTO would get involved.

A final important point to remember about the WTO's focus on international trade is that it does not contemplate economic sanctions being used as a tool of foreign policy to pressure countries against behaving in a manner that is contrary to the interests of global security. Economic sanctions, which tend to be authorized by the United Nations or other international organizations such as NATO, are effectively bans on the export of certain goods to certain countries, most recently Russia (because of the Crimean annexation) and North Korea and Iran (because of their nuclear weapons programmes). These are clearly an affront to liberalized international trade. Goods that would normally be available in these places are no longer because of legal barriers.

The WTO does not get involved with these types of trade barriers because they are not economic in nature, in the sense that they are not intended to advantage domestic producers over foreign ones. They are expressly aimed at coercing a country to adopt policies that are more in keeping with world peace, such as nuclear non-proliferation and the respect of sovereign states' territorial integrity.

The WTO openly acknowledges in several of its agreements that it will cooperate with economic sanction programmes, such as those authorized by the UN Security Council. It also recognizes that its rules on international trade are subordinate to the interests of national and global security. While one of the ideological foundations for free trade is the notion that countries which trade with each other do not go to war with each other, sometimes shutting off the supply of certain goods (especially luxury items that are favoured by evil dictators) is the best way to force a country to stop doing dangerous things without resorting to actual military intervention. This is why it is unlikely that Russia would be able to use the WTO dispute settlement system to challenge the sanctions imposed on it.

With what is in essence a remarkably limited mandate over international trade, in its simplest form the WTO is very much like any other organization that is composed of individuals acting collectively to reach decisions. Public institutions like governments with voting legislatures and an executive manager operate this way in order to administer the functioning of society on behalf of their citizens. Private commercial bodies like corporations have a similar purpose and structure – with a board of directors as well as a CEO who performs a role not dissimilar to that of the WTO's Director-General – acting to serve the interests of their shareholders.

While the WTO is not particularly unique in terms of its organizational structure, nor broad in terms of its focus, it is genuinely groundbreaking in its instrumentation – by which I mean its rules on free trade. The WTO agreements, which form the constitution that binds the members together under a common framework, are the essential tools by which the WTO fulfils its mandate to enlarge and preserve global trade. Whether it succeeds or fails in this goal depends directly on the obligations contained in these agreements. In the next chapter we will turn our attention to the WTO's main legal principles, its three central pillars.

2

The three pillars: the principles of tariff reduction, non-discrimination and transparency

There are many treaties, agreements, statements and policy instruments that comprise the rules of membership of the WTO. Some trade lawyers as well as economists and diplomats make a very good living becoming well acquainted with all or at least most of them. But at their core, the obligations entailed by membership of the WTO can be reduced to three fairly simple principles. These three rules were enshrined in the original GATT agreement created in the 1940s, and are now seen in many of the organization's more specific legal provisions.

The first of these principles is that the member states agree to stick to their tariff commitments as defined during the negotiation process I mentioned in the previous chapter. Second, members must not discriminate against goods on the basis of their country of origin when their governments implement various laws. Finally, members promise that they will be as open and clear as possible when creating and enforcing these laws.

Tariff commitments

Tariffs are extra fees placed upon goods as they cross international borders. They are essentially customs duties charged on imports by governmental officials that must be paid as a condition of entry of the good into the foreign country. In many countries where income tax is insignificant because wages are themselves low, tariffs can represent an important source of revenue for governments. In these cases, tariffs can be an instrument of national economic policy.

The WTO prefers tariffs to quotas, which are prohibited under the GATT. Quotas are quantitative restrictions on the total amount of a given good which can be imported, and they are forbidden because they do not lead to revenue like tariffs do. Quotas are also harder to detect because, unlike with a price increase linked to a tariff, consumers aren't as aware of the effect of a decrease in supply on the ultimate price they pay. They are also believed to be less conducive to gradual elimination through negotiation than tariffs are. In contrast, customs duties are relatively easy to collect, which can also be advantageous for developing (low-income) states, although in most developed (wealthy) countries tariffs are only a marginal source of governmental income. Over the years the WTO (and the GATT before it) compelled member countries to convert quotas into tariffs, essentially forbidding them from imposing a limit on the total amount of imported goods, but allowing them to add charges to imports. Economists even created a word for this – tariffication. Among the most well known of the quotas that were eliminated as a consequence of the WTO were those relating to the import of textiles and clothing, resulting in the massive influx of Chinese-made apparel into the West that we have grown accustomed to.

One of the main purposes of tariffs is to make foreign goods artificially more expensive. This gives domestic producers an advantage when competing for local consumers. Of course, eliminating distortions like this is one of the WTO's primary goals. The substantial reduction in tariffs is a key means by which the WTO helps to ensure that there is a level playing field on international markets for goods. It is estimated that the possible

annual increase in global gross domestic product (GDP) resulting from ongoing WTO negotiations on the reduction of tariffs
such as customs duties is US $63 billion. Much of these gains are
expected to be enjoyed by developing countries, making tariff
reduction a key strategy in the eradication of global poverty. As a
result of negotiations under the GATT since the 1940s, the average duty on industrial (meaning manufactured) goods imposed
by developed countries has dropped from around forty percent
to about four percent today. Economists tend to agree that tariff
levels below five percent should be viewed as a nuisance rather
than as a barrier to trade.

The fact that some tariffs exist at all shows that they are
not illegal under the WTO's rules. Member states are allowed to
impose them, so long as the level of tariffs on each specific good
is not higher than what was committed to in trade negotiations.
These committed levels of tariffs are called 'bound' – meaning the
amount, usually expressed as a percentage of value (ad valorem),
although sometimes a percentage of weight, of a given good that
each state will charge on imports as they enter its territory. Each
type of good has its own bound rate. Under the GATT (one of
the chief system of rules within the WTO), all WTO members
must commit to sticking to their bound tariffs. This means that
if a country ever imposes a customs duty that is higher than its
bound tariff rate, the country from which that good originates
may allege that its rights have been infringed. This doesn't prevent
a country from imposing a tariff that is lower than its bound
rate, which can also happen on occasion. Each member country
of the WTO maintains a list of the rates for a whole range of
imported products. These documents, called Schedules of Tariff
Concessions, can be several thousand pages long. For developed
countries, more than ninety-nine percent of product lines are
now covered by bound tariffs (up from seventy-eight percent in
previous decades). In developing countries about three quarters
of goods have bound tariffs.

So, although discouraged, tariffs can be seen as an instrument of protectionism that is generally allowed under WTO rules. Members are free to use tariffs to structure the needs of their domestic economy, and to address the vulnerability of particular industries. Although tariff levels have dropped considerably since their heyday in the mid-twentieth century, there remain disturbingly high tariffs on goods in some sensitive sectors, most notably agriculture and textiles. These barriers are highly controversial, and are the source of much ongoing tension among WTO members during negotiations. The idea is that members will continue to negotiate for lower and lower tariffs, with a view to eliminating them completely one day. Much progress has already been made: tariffs are no longer the chief source of protectionism in world trade.

If one WTO member believes that a good which it exports has been charged a tariff higher than the importing country's bound rate, it can bring a claim through the WTO courts, in a procedure that we'll take a closer look at in the next chapter. For now, it is enough to know that this will entail an investigation into exactly what tariff each country committed to in its Schedule of Concessions. For example, the EU got away with charging a higher tariff on chicken cuts because it had reclassified a certain type of boneless chicken under a product heading that carried a heavier tariff. It put the relevant product under the 'poultry: fresh, chilled or frozen' category instead of the 'meat: salted, in brine, dried or smoked' category, while it could arguably have fitted under either. This was a crafty strategy but, importantly, it was not illegal.

The WTO also establishes rules on the way in which customs duties on incoming goods must be applied by governments. These relate to the correct classification of the imported good which allows customs authorities to determine which duty to levy; the assessment of the value of the imported good; and finally, rules on how to establish the origin of the particular good. This material can be quite technical, requiring interpretation by experts, but it's important because it ensures that tariffs are imposed in a manner that is consistent with the commitments undertaken by a member through negotiations. Rules of origin can be particularly difficult to apply because of the increasingly sophisticated supply chains associated with highly manufactured goods like cars, where parts can come from all over the world. The multiple components found in so many modern goods make it hard to establish definitely where a particular finished product actually comes from and therefore what its bound rate should be.

Non-discrimination as to origin

Charges imposed at the border are not the only way countries can make foreign goods artificially more expensive. They can impose a whole raft of regulations on products from overseas that give them a disadvantage vis-à-vis the local equivalent. It is this concept of equivalence that forms the basis of the second pillar of the WTO – the prohibition of discrimination.

If one morning you went to make coffee only to discover that you had run out, would you have tea instead? They're both hot beverages and you probably pour them into the same cup. Chances are you use the same milk and sugar to flavour them. Isn't one as good as the other? Not really. They taste completely different for one. Coffee has a higher caffeine content (unless it's decaffeinated). Coffee probably takes a bit longer to brew (unless you like instant), although if you're into pots and strainers, tea brewing can be quite a chore too. If you think deciding between tea and coffee is easy enough, what about choosing between different brands of coffee, let's say Nescafé or Maxwell House? Are brands of coffee really different drinks, or just different flavours of what is essentially the same product? To take a classic example of brand differentiation, it's unlikely that you have ever seen someone turn down Pepsi in a restaurant when they asked for Coke. Most people would agree that Coke and Pepsi do have distinctive tastes, but few would argue that they are so different that they can't be substituted for one another, or that one should carry a higher sales tax than the other. After all, they're both soft drinks.

Clearly the concept of equivalence or 'likeness' can become quite complicated, especially with all of the variations in products and services that we now enjoy. But it is crucial to the WTO's rules that prohibit discrimination. This is because when a country imposes a trade barrier, for example such as a sales tax, it is only illegal when it is applied to a product from one place and not to another similar one from somewhere else. This would be discrimination based on origin – one of the main impediments to globalization.

While discriminatory treatment may be helpful to the manufacturers of those products which get the better treatment, it doesn't make any economic sense, especially in the long term. It distorts markets in favour of goods and services that are either more expensive or of lower quality – sometimes both. One of the WTO's main goals is to make sure that discrimination – in the form of unfair national laws – does not take place. So consumers are able to buy the things that offer the most value for money, not those which are artificially cheaper because some country has decided to say that they are. The WTO does this through two important principles: national treatment and most favoured nation, both of which are enshrined in the GATT.

National treatment means that governments must not impose any requirements on foreign goods that are not placed on domestic goods. So a tariff, tax or sales requirement that applies to a foreign product must also apply to the equivalent domestic product. Most favoured nation requires that governments must not impose different legal requirements on goods coming from different countries. Goods must be treated the same regardless of the foreign country from which they originate. This prevents favouritism or strategic alliances among countries. So any reduction in tariffs or taxes extended to goods from one place must be extended to goods from all places. One of the key exceptions to most favoured nation relates to regional trade agreements, such as the EU, which grants preferential terms to goods originating within its borders. We will have a closer look at these types of arrangements, which the WTO expressly permits, below.

But, as I explained above, both these rules hinge on the products being the same, or in the language of the GATT 'like'. The comparison between the levels of treatment of two products doesn't have any meaning if the products are not the same. An exporter of tyres from Brazil can't allege discrimination based on the tariff level imposed on Brazilian apples by the European Union. Tyres aren't apples. But he might legitimately complain if tyres from his country get a higher tariff under the European Union's laws than tyres from Thailand.

In the mid-1990s, the multinational banana company Chiquita lobbied the US government to bring a complaint at the WTO about the European Union's import regime on bananas. Europe imposed a higher tariff rate as well as quotas on bananas that Chiquita (as well as other smaller companies) sourced mostly from Latin American countries like Guatemala and Honduras than it did on bananas grown in former European colonies like the Ivory Coast and Cameroon. The WTO court decided the dispute in favour of the US government. Key to the court's finding that Europe's import regime discriminated against Latin American bananas was the recognition that bananas from one country were the same as bananas from another country. In other words there was no justification for placing a different tariff or quota on bananas from one place than on bananas from another place.

This ruling makes sense from a practical viewpoint – while bananas might taste and look different depending on how ripe they are (yellow and soft, or green and firm) a banana is a banana no matter where it's from. There is no Coke and Pepsi of the banana world. It also makes sense from an economic point of view. Europe's charging different tariffs and imposing quotas had a clear political motivation, which although noble (helping their former colonies) was unfair to other countries and, more importantly, it skewed the world market for bananas. Consumers in Europe bought bananas from Africa instead of from Latin America, even though Latin American farmers were able to produce them at lower cost, and thus growers in Latin America had fewer customers.

It took another dispute, this time involving the tax treatment by the government of Japan of a locally produced alcoholic beverage called shochu, for the WTO court to come up with a more workable test for likeness in less clear-cut cases. The issue was whether a Japanese law that taxed foreign alcoholic beverages like vodka at a higher rate than shochu violated the national treatment guarantee of the GATT, which was binding on Japan as a member of the WTO. Liquor distillers in Canada, the US and the European Union had encouraged their respective governments to challenge the Japanese law through the WTO courts. These three are among the leading exporters of spirits in the world, with Japan as one of the biggest markets, accounting for several billion US dollars in sales. Of course, it's up to Japan to tax whatever it wants at whatever rate, as long as it does so evenly. But this looked like a case of protectionism.

Shochu, a clear, strong alcoholic beverage distilled in Japan from potatoes, rice or other grains, is quite popular in the domestic market, enjoying higher sales at home than the more internationally well-known Japanese drink sake. It has similar characteristics to liquors from other parts of the world, most notably vodka. Why then should shochu be taxed at a lower rate? The WTO court ruled against Japan, which had attempted to justify the lower tax on shochu on the basis of its distinctive taste and ingredients. But according to the court, other than the drink's different filtration process, foreign vodka was essentially identical to shochu, meaning that the higher tax was an instance of illegal discrimination against a like product.

In deciding this case, the court clarified that an assessment of 'likeness' for the purposes of evaluating national treatment would be done on a case-by-case basis. The concept of likeness therefore could expand and contract like an accordion – a famous image that is now part of the standard arsenal of international trade lawyers. This brings flexibility to the likeness test that can be quite useful when making the case for or against a country's laws. At the same time the accordion model isn't very helpful in setting a stable, predictable rule to assess all laws affecting all goods around the world going forward. How can an exporter know whether or not its particular product will be considered 'like' something else that gets better treatment under a national law if the meaning keeps shifting?

Fortunately the court in the shochu case did give lawyers and their clients a set of practical guidelines that can assist in establishing whether a good is like another good for the purposes of the non-discrimination tests. These are: the product's end use in a given market (liquors are fundamentally beverages meant to be consumed by humans in liquid form); consumers' tastes and habits (people buy varieties of alcoholic beverages in certain quantities at certain times and at certain prices compared to other beverages and even other alcoholic beverages); and the product's properties (taste, colour, alcohol content and ingredients). So while the answer to each of these three questions is one of fact to be determined by people who conduct market research and not by lawyers, the test itself, known as the Japan Alcohol test, is very much a fixture in the international trade law firmament. The WTO court used this test to determine that shochu was like vodka because it had similar end uses for consumers (the same type of customers bought both products in similar patterns), and they shared most physical characteristics (colour, ingredients, taste). Other alcoholic beverages such as gin were not like shochu because gin used additives; rum had different ingredients and brandy looked different. It is remarkable that pivotal issues of international law come down to decisions not much different to those made by people doing their weekend shopping!

Another WTO court looking at the differential taxation of alcoholic beverages, this time imposed by South Korea in favour of its local liquor soju, summed up the 'likeness' issue by concluding that the test was really meant to evaluate whether or not the two products in question were actually, as well as potentially, in competition with each other. Soju is a clear colourless spirit made from grain, and under South Korean law it enjoyed much lower rates of tax than foreign drinks like brandy and gin. This treatment seriously undermined actual as well as anticipated future exports of various liquors like gin and whisky to South Korea, another of the world's largest markets for alcoholic beverages distilled in Europe, the US and Canada. South Korea lost the dispute and had to straighten out its tax on alcoholic beverages.

So, if you are in the mood for tea but coffee will do, then tea and coffee are fundamentally competing products, so we can say that they are like. But if you really want a cupcake and the muffin next to it simply will not do, then cupcakes are not like muffins even though they sort of look the same and both go well with coffee in the afternoon. In economics this is called elasticity of substitution – when you run out of something, how willing are you to switch to something else, even if you haven't tried it yet but might if you are given the opportunity? Of course this behaviour will depend on the tastes and preferences of average consumers, not coffee or cupcake addicts.

It's important to recognize that the non-discrimination test created by the WTO courts is about the effect of the national law, not the intent. The difference in effects- versus intent-based approaches to discrimination is an exceedingly difficult and technical one that continues to draw much attention from the

WTO courts. Generally speaking, it doesn't matter what the Japanese or South Korean governments intended to achieve, whether it was the sinister urge to destroy foreign competition in the alcoholic beverage industry or it was purely accidental. What matters is how it affected foreign spirits producers' ability to enter the domestic markets and compete against shochu and soju in appealing to Japanese and Korean alcohol drinkers. So when it comes to free trade, it's not important if a government resents the fact that its people want things that come from other places – under the national treatment and most favoured nation rules, all that matters is that the foreign good is not treated the same as the local one, or that a foreign good from one place is not treated better than the same good from another place. In order to help resolve this problem, the WTO has special rules of origin which standardize and simplify the way each country's customs authorities verify the origin of various goods for the purpose of imposing tariffs and other regulations.

One of the reasons for the effects-based focus of the non-discrimination rule is that the practical impact of discrimination is what hits a company's bottom line, not their hurt feelings. The other, perhaps more prosaic reason for concentrating on the effects of a trade law is that it is almost impossible to find out why governments really do anything. If you don't believe that, watch any politician attempt to answer a direct question and see how skilfully they get out of providing any answer, let alone an honest or credible one. Of course, when a government actually admits that its intention in imposing a discriminatory trade regulation was protectionism, as a member of the Mexican Congress once did when he stated that the purpose of a tax on foreign soft drinks was to shield the local sugar cane industry, this will not be ignored by judges.

Another key component of the national treatment and most favoured nation rules is that the treatment is actually less favourable, meaning that it is in some way damaging. Being different on its own isn't enough to violate international law. This issue came before a WTO court examining another South Korean law, this time affecting beef. As anyone who has been to a Korean restaurant knows, Koreans are big on beef. But not just their own beef – Koreans love imported beef, particularly from the US.

The South Korean government imposed a law insisting that imported beef be sold in separate stores to domestic beef. Only small retailers were allowed to sell foreign beef and only large ones allowed to sell domestic beef, with some large stores permitted to sell small quantities of foreign beef if it was displayed in a separate, designated section of the store. This enraged US farmers, who felt that their frozen and fresh beef exports, which were identical to the local variety, couldn't compete fairly in their third-largest market – South Korea. The WTO court ruled that the South Korean sales law restricted the choice available to consumers. It made it harder for them to get foreign beef over domestic beef, unfairly disadvantaging the equivalent imported product. This was a sound ruling – clearly it would annoy people to have to make separate trips to a boutique deli to get US beef when they had done most of their weekly grocery shopping somewhere else. Why not just get the local stuff, and save yourself the inconvenience?

In deciding this dispute between the US and South Korea, the WTO court also drew an interesting and influential distinction between open discrimination and indirect or hidden discrimination. Where discrimination is open (foreign beef is openly treated differently to domestic beef), you still have to show that the treatment is worse, as it was in this case because the inconvenience to shoppers would encourage them to buy the local product. So, if foreign beef had to be sold in red packages and domestic beef in blue packages, this wouldn't mean that there was *worse* treatment, unless of course red packages were more expensive, or there was some evidence that consumers didn't like red packaging.

The court in the Korea beef dispute added that the non-discrimination rule would also apply to indirect or disguised discrimination. This would occur where the treatment under national law of the foreign and domestic product is formally the same but ends up being different (and worse) without any obvious mention of national origin. So, for example, if South Korea had placed a restricted sales requirement on beef from a type of cow that was found only in the US but not on beef from cows from Korea, without actually referring to their origin in the wording of the law, then this would still be discrimination (given that it satisfied the likeness test too). A law like this would delight South Korean farmers but would upset quite a few people in Texas. It would also obviously irritate meat lovers in Seoul by boosting the price of the all-you-can-eat deals at the barbecue restaurants. Simply put, you can't hide protectionism by finding an indirect way of harming a foreign product without actually saying you are doing so.

The GATT's national treatment requirement often draws the anger of anti-globalizationalists, many of them right wing as well as left wing, because it affects 'behind the border' regulations, meaning all kinds of laws enacted by governments that may affect that particular product, not just taxes as the good enters the country. Some of these internal laws, like conditions of sale, can have very important policy purposes that countries are reluctant to surrender to the whims of international courts like those of the WTO. We'll come back to some of these issues, like health, the environment and animal rights, in chapter 5.

In contrast, the most favoured nation requirement does not step so heavily on a country's toes because it doesn't require a comparison to domestic goods. The comparison is between the treatment of two (or more) foreign goods. So in that sense it is probably the least controversial of the WTO's non-discrimination rules, at least in terms of each country's ability to control its own economy. The most favoured nation rule is contentious for a different reason – it prevents cliques from forming in international economic relations, and in so doing it preserves globalization over regionalism. When you were a child and you had a party, your mother may have told you that you had to invite all of your classmates or you were not allowed to have a party at all. While we may not have liked this rule at the time, we now know that it was meant to protect the feelings of the one or two kids who otherwise wouldn't have been invited and who then would have felt left out.

But what about your really close friends? What if you want to have a little get-together with just a few of your best pals – you can't know everyone in the class that well, and we know that being really close to a few people or one special person is one of the nicest parts of friendship. What is true of personal relationships is also true of international trade and diplomatic relationships. The WTO knew from its creation in the mid-1990s that many countries were already forming regional trade blocs

REGIONAL TRADE AGREEMENTS (RTAs)

In recent years, the stalled negotiations at the WTO have led commentators to urge that the future of free trade is in bilateralism, not multilateralism. Indeed, almost six hundred RTAs, meaning reciprocal trade agreements between two or more countries, have been notified to the WTO. Many more are expected in the coming years, including the trillion-dollar Transatlantic Trade and Investment Partnership and the Trans-Pacific Partnership (governing investment as well as trade). Asian countries are particularly fond of these arrangements, with China indicating recently that it sees bilateral agreements as more effective in furthering its economic interests than the WTO, where consensus among 161 countries is becoming extremely difficult. The North American Free Trade Agreement (NAFTA) and the European Union are two of the most important examples of successful regional trade agreements. NAFTA is a free trade zone which means that tariffs on goods that move between the three members of Canada, the US and Mexico are the same, although each country's external tariffs to the rest of the world may be different. The European Union is a common market for goods, services and investment throughout all the twenty-eight independent European countries that belong to it, as well as a significant political organization. It has common internal tariffs (all members treat each other's goods the same) as well as common external tariffs (all members treat outsiders the same). NAFTA and the EU, as well as many other similar arrangements, have been able to negotiate lower tariffs on goods than those achieved by the WTO. They have also extended non-discrimination promises to cover other matters like investment, often using language taken directly from the old GATT of 1947.

with one another – effectively giving special treatment, such as lower tariffs, to goods coming from certain countries and not from others. This reflects the reality that it is often easier for a small group of countries to negotiate treaties of any kind than it is for countries to do so globally at the WTO.

Regional trade blocs are incompatible with the everyone-is-equal mentality of the WTO. How can separate groupings be reconciled with a global trade organization like the WTO, in particular the most favoured nation provision where all countries promise to treat everyone the same and not have special friends? Canada and the US are having a party and New Zealand isn't invited.

The answer is a crucial exception to the rule that you must not discriminate. This is the preferential trade agreement exception alluded to above. It allows countries to form trading blocs and to give better treatment to goods originating from within that bloc than to goods coming from outside of it. The WTO allows this because its main goal is the reduction in barriers to trade – not to consolidate its own grip over the global economy at all costs. So, if a regional arrangement can achieve lower barriers (there is much economic debate as to whether regional arrangements actually are economically productive), then the WTO will give it its blessing.

But there are a few requirements. First, the overall level of trade barrier within the regional grouping must not be higher or more restrictive than it was before. Second, the trade barriers levied against non-members of the regional grouping must not be raised because of it. And finally, you have to tell the WTO about it and let it give its stamp of approval, which it basically always does because it's almost impossible to verify whether or not the first two requirements have not been met by the bloc.

It's still not as easy as it sounds, especially for customs unions like the European Union where there must be a common external tariff from all countries within it on a given good. So Spain and Germany (inside the union) have to make sure that they have the same tariff level on steel coming from South Africa (outside the union). But what happens if, before joining the union, Germany's tariff on steel from South Africa was lower than it was after joining the union? It will have to raise its tariff on South African steel to get to the same level as Spain, France and the rest of Europe, a key requirement of entry into the union. This looks anti-trade, and it could obviously upset South African steelmakers seeking to sell to German builders.

Something like that might never happen – but it turns out that it did. Turkey was preparing to join Europe's common market (although it did not become a full member of the European Union). Like a college fraternity requiring that all members get the same tattoo, Turkey had to impose quotas on clothing products so that it came into line with levels imposed by the rest of Europe. The problem for Turkey was that it had never imposed any clothing quotas on any countries. When Turkey did this as part of its initiation into the club of Europe, India, with its vibrant textile industry, complained to the WTO.

The WTO court resolved the dispute by looking at the word 'necessary', which appears in the text of the GATT. The court said that the country imposing the barrier (Turkey putting in place quotas on clothes from India and other places outside Europe) had to show that the requirements to join the union could not be met without imposing that barrier. The trade restriction must be absolutely necessary, or else the customs union can't be formed.

Turkey wasn't able to demonstrate that the quota was essential because there were other ways that it could have upheld Europe's customs requirements for foreign clothes without imposing quotas on Indian clothes. Specifically, the court said that Turkey could have imposed labelling requirements on Indian clothes so that when Turkish exporters subsequently sold clothes in Europe, ones originating from within the union (including Turkey) would have one label, and those coming from outside (places like India) would not. Turkey didn't do this, so the quotas imposed on India were unnecessary and had to be removed, much to the delight of textile companies in India.

Transparency

When a supplier is thinking about exporting goods to a particular country, it has to know precisely what tariff levels will be imposed as well as what other conditions, such as sales taxes, conditions of sale and so on, will be placed on its goods in order to determine whether or not it can make a profit from the venture. This means that it needs to know the trade rules of the destination country. But this information is only available if that country has been willing to share it with the rest of the world in a manner that is accessible and understandable. This brings us to the third and final central pillar of the WTO – transparency. WTO members must be as open and clear as possible when enacting laws that affect international trade.

The WTO has rules and procedures to ensure that confusion relating to the laws affecting traded goods is minimized. These include rules about publishing all trade-related laws, notifying other WTO members when new laws are created or modified and, finally, the establishment within each member country of special offices, called 'enquiry points', that are available to respond to requests for information. The WTO itself conducts reviews of each member's overall regime of trade laws in its periodic trade policy review process, and publishes these results on its website. So in that sense, the WTO is also an important collector and disseminator of information about the rules of trade operating in each of its member countries.

When member countries fall foul of these rules, for example when the European Union took eight months to update its official bulletin of trade laws about changes affecting the trade in information technology-oriented products, or when the US changed its import regime on underwear before it spelled it out in its official documents, they can get in trouble with the WTO authorities. We'll come to exactly what getting in trouble means in the next chapter, but for now it's enough to be aware that the transparency requirements aren't idle suggestions, but actual binding laws imposed on all of the WTO's members. It may not seem like a big deal, but if your business is exporting socks and boxers to the US, you should be able to find out what kind of customs duties you will face before you ship them across the ocean, not when they're being unloaded at the dock.

Improvement in the transparency of governmental regulations is thought to be one of the added benefits of WTO membership, beyond just lowering tariffs and preventing discrimination. In addition to stripping away some of the confusion associated with exporting goods abroad, cleaning up the red tape of excessive or messy bureaucracy can help local businesses as well as foreign ones, benefiting the overall economy. When Russia joined the WTO in 2012, many business people in Moscow were hopeful that it would usher in a new era of openness and fair dealings for an economy that had been crippled by corruption. It's not clear yet whether the WTO has had that effect on Russia, but it's fairly obvious that China has benefited from the WTO's no-nonsense approach to governmental inefficiency and back-door dealings. China shot up the world rankings in ease of doing business following its accession to the WTO in 2001, in no small part because of WTO rules on transparency. It is now substantially less onerous to start a business, pay taxes, enforce contracts and get compensation from the government in China than it was even a short time ago. The same is true for many other emerging markets and countries making the transition from communism.

For developing countries, the WTO principle of transparency has another key dimension, and one that has become an important part of the organization's recent negotiations in Bali. Trade facilitation is the WTO term for improvements in the practical aspects associated with goods crossing international borders, meaning procedures involved with clearing customs, like checking cargo and collecting duties. While these activities have been reduced to an efficient minimum in most developed states, customs procedures at border crossings in Africa can be a nightmare, sometimes adding as much as fifty percent to the cost of trade, mostly due to delay and bribes. With WTO best-practice guidance and monitoring, it is expected that these expenses will be drastically reduced. For example, the time it takes goods to cross the Uganda–Kenya border is expected to drop from almost two days to only seven hours, thanks to WTO-instigated transparency and efficiencies. This is not just about convenience – perishable goods like food will go bad in unrefrigerated trucks after two days. Cameroon alone is expected to gain more than US $25 million per year by cleaning up its border procedures to conform to WTO requirements.

The WTO's central principles of tariff commitments, non-discrimination and transparency do not operate in isolation from one another – the fact that they are interrelated makes them even more effective in controlling protectionism. Bound tariffs must be extended on a non-discriminatory basis to like imports from all countries, just as all trade-related laws, whether tariffs or internal measures, must be conveyed in an accessible, understandable fashion. Working in tandem, these three pillars are able to do away with most (but not all) barriers to the free flow of goods around the world. But how are these rules applied in practice, and what happens when there are disagreements about if, or how, they have been broken?

3
In the courtroom: the WTO dispute settlement system

Unlike the WTO's main function as a forum for negotiations, which has been fraught with difficulties and lack of progress, especially recently, the dispute settlement system has been immensely successful, sometimes referred to as 'the jewel in the crown' among the WTO's many internal bodies. It is the most active international tribunal in the world, hearing more disputes by far than either the International Court of Justice of the United Nations or the International Criminal Court. The WTO dispute settlement system has enabled the relatively smooth implementation of the WTO's many agreements among its 161 members for 20 years, and is a model of how an international court should function in terms of efficiency, reach and upholding the rule of law. In fact, many commentators have urged that the WTO's court system should be expanded to hear non-trade-related matters, like competition law, investment and even environmental matters, simply because it has worked so well. Still, the system is not without it flaws.

This chapter will explain how the WTO dispute settlement system functions, what it does for world trade and some of the ongoing concerns about how it could be improved to better serve the interests of the WTO members, traders and ordinary citizens.

Structure: panels and Appellate Body

It's been said that disputes at the WTO are really about broken promises. If one member country believes that its rights, as outlined in one of the various WTO agreements, have been infringed by another member, then it can try to reach a settlement through informal discussions. If this doesn't work, the injured member can bring a claim through the dispute settlement process, which is essentially a court of law that decides whether or not a member's rights have been infringed. We've already seen some examples of this in the previous chapter about the 'likeness' issue and non-discrimination. The purpose of the dispute settlement system is to prevent members from taking action unilaterally, for example by imposing trade sanctions or raising tariffs against the member they feel has hurt them. This can be disastrous, because it can lead to the escalation of tit-for-tat aggression, ultimately defeating the whole purpose of having a global organization that eliminates barriers to trade.

It was precisely this type of 'aggressive unilateralism', especially by the US, which caused trade diplomats to realize that the old GATT way of resolving disputes, through informal meetings where no binding decisions were reached, was just not working. So, when the WTO was created in 1995, trade representatives from each country agreed that a new formal, rules-based system of binding dispute settlement was needed; one where a decision would be rendered by an unbiased panel of experts, and that decision would have legal consequences for the parties to the dispute. Negotiators came up with the brilliant idea of 'reverse consensus'. The rulings of these panels (euphemistically called recommendations, because it sounds less intrusive into national autonomy) would be automatically accepted as binding by the WTO community, unless there was a unanimous decision *not* to accept them. So, unlike the previous pre-WTO situation, where one GATT signatory could block a ruling that went against its interests, now decisions of the panels would be accepted virtually automatically. It is practically inconceivable that every one of the 161 member countries would resist a panel ruling. Decisions of the panels now had significant legal implications.

The modern panel process created along with the WTO also offers other vital improvements to the resolution of disputes under the previous GATT system. Now, disputes have strict time frames, preventing them from dragging on for years as they often did before. While WTO disputes have flexible time frames for each stage, disputes should normally not take more than a year and are often resolved much quicker in urgent cases. The disputes themselves are now more legal, focusing on the specific obligations raised by each of the WTO's agreements. The procedure is often described as 'litigation', using American-style legal language, and indeed they can be quite adversarial with evidence, argument and counter-argument as in a traditional courtroom. A number of high-price US law firms have developed specialities in bringing (or defending) WTO claims, although it remains a decidedly niche area in the practice of international law.

Consultations aimed at resolving disputes before the instigation of formal legal proceedings are still mandatory, in keeping with the WTO's ethos of achieving diplomatic solutions where possible. During consultations parties talk to each other to see if they can settle their differences on their own, sometimes asking the Director-General of the WTO to step in and act as a mediator. Parties are encouraged to continue to attempt to 'settle out of court' during all stages of the dispute settlement process. If initial attempts to resolve the matter informally fail, the next stage of the process, which is undertaken if consultations have failed after sixty days, is the appointment of a panel. The two adversarial parties in the case have forty-five days to appoint the panel and the panel itself gets six months to hear and decide the dispute. As mentioned above, the panel's report can only be rejected by consensus of every WTO member, so its decisions, while termed recommendations, are practically impossible to overturn: they have the same practical effect as a binding ruling of an ordinary domestic court. The panel's report is normally given to the parties to the dispute within six months.

The panel stage should be done in roughly a year – which is virtually light speed to most court systems around the world. But the quickness of the WTO panel process comes at a cost. It is often suggested that there isn't enough time for cases to be properly argued and for all evidence to be heard. Still, most agree that the dispute settlement system strikes a good balance between efficiency and justice. In fact, the WTO dispute settlement system is often described as a model for judicial proceedings at the international level. Better to get to the heart of the matter and get it out of the way than let the whole thing drag on for years, bogged down by irrelevancies. In practice, panel proceedings often do exceed the standard time frames – the average length from beginning to end is actually fifteen months. This is because of difficulties associated with scheduling meetings, other administrative matters like translating documents and also because of the increased use of experts.

Panels hold their hearings at the WTO headquarters in Geneva and are normally composed of three people, although five can be used if the parties request it. Panellists must be well qualified and have experience of being involved in WTO disputes. As with most judicial positions on courts and tribunals around the world, panellists must also be independent and impartial (essentially meaning not linked to either of the parties' governments), and they are normally not nationals of either of the parties to the dispute, although this can be waived by agreement. So far, panellists tend to be current or retired government or trade officials with a background in law. To assist in the selection of panellists, the WTO maintains a list of individuals who possess the required qualifications to serve as panellists, although you do not have to be on the list to be a panellist.

After a panel has rendered its decision on the dispute, either party can appeal it. Sometimes both sides do. About seventy percent of panel reports have been appealed. Appeals must be based on points of law, like the interpretation of a legal issue (such as the 'likeness' issue that we discussed in the previous chapter). Appeals are heard by three members of a permanent seven-member Appellate Body, which also sits in Geneva. The Appellate Body, which is sometimes described in the media as the 'World Trade Court', can uphold, modify or reverse the panel's legal findings and conclusions. The appeals process normally lasts less than sixty days, with an absolute maximum of ninety days. The WTO members must then accept the Appellate Body's recommendation, again unless there is reverse consensus not to – which means that the rulings are basically always adopted as binding. There is no further appeal stage from here, giving both finality as well as useful oversight to the process of dispute settlement at the WTO.

Like panellists, the seven Appellate Body members must be recognized experts with proven experience in international trade law and able to exercise independent judgment. They must not be affiliated with any government, and must not pursue any professional activities that are inconsistent with their duties and responsibilities. The expertise required by Appellate Body members should allow them to resolve issues of law covered in the panel report. Appeals do not rehear the case; they settle disagreements surrounding the legal interpretation of provisions of the WTO agreements, like the GATT, as well as the other ones that we will look at later in this book. Appellate Body membership should be broadly representative of the membership of the WTO itself, which means that the individuals should be drawn from the various geographical areas, levels of development and legal systems of the world. The current seven members are from India, Belgium,

South Korea, the United States, Mexico, South Africa and China. Appellate Body members are appointed for terms of four years, which can be renewed once, like the US Presidency. The decision to appoint Appellate Body members is reached by representatives of each member country of the WTO by consensus.

The Appellate Body hears appeals in divisions of three members, and the members are chosen on the basis of rotation. So it is essentially random which particular Appellate Body member ends up hearing a particular appeal. Unlike the panel process, Appellate Body members can sit in cases where their

PETER VAN DEN BOSSCHE, MEMBER OF THE APPELLATE BODY

Professor Peter Van den Bossche is one of the seven current members of the WTO's standing Appellate Body (the phrase 'judge' is not used, although they are regularly described as such in the media). He was reappointed for a second four-year term in 2013, as decided at a meeting in Geneva by all existing members of the WTO. During his first four years as a member of the Appellate Body, Van den Bossche issued judgments in several high-profile disputes, including one relating to tens of billions of euros of alleged European subsidies to the aircraft manufacturer Airbus, as well as a dispute regarding the controversial US prohibition on the sales of clove-flavoured cigarettes. Before he was appointed to the WTO's top court, Peter Van den Bossche worked as a legal secretary for the European Court of Justice, and was counsellor at the WTO Appellate Body Secretariat (an office which provides legal and administrative support to the Appellate Body itself), later serving as the Acting Director of the Secretariat. A national of Belgium, he studied law at the University of Antwerp, the University of Michigan and the European University Institute in Florence, where he obtained his PhD. In addition to teaching law at the World Trade Institute in Berne, the University of Barcelona and the China–EU School of Law in Beijing, since 1992 Peter Van den Bossche has been a professor of law at Maastricht University, where he teaches world trade law and also graciously supervises a number of PhD students, including a certain law lecturer from Canada who wrote this book.

countries of origin are party. However, when the Appellate Body renders its decision, it is the decision of the whole division. There are not separate opinions presented by each member, like in many domestic court systems. This anonymity can shelter a member from backlash from their own government if they end up rendering a decision that is against its interest. As with the panels, the divisions of the Appellate Body make every effort to render a decision by consensus, but if this fails they will take a majority vote.

How decisions are made

As with legal proceedings in any court, panels and Appellate Body hearings have rules about the way trials are conducted and about how the judges must make their decisions. The legalism of WTO dispute settlement reports as well as the way in which they are made is partially due to the presence of a team of legal experts within the WTO that assists panels in rendering their decision. There are divisions of experts for special types of disputes, who also help out panels with highly technical matters. The formalism is also a result of WTO members seeking predictable outcomes to their disputes, in contrast with the fuzzy diplomatic procedure of the early GATT days when panel recommendations were based on informal discussions and often couched in vague suggestions that were intended not to offend anyone. The most obvious formalism is in the time frames, but there are other rules that are crucial to the way the panels and Appellate Body conduct their business.

One important rule governs exactly what the appeals court is allowed to consider. When the Appellate Body reviews decisions of the panels these must relate to issues of law, not fact. Questions arising regarding whether an event occurred or did not occur are questions of fact and they should rightly be assessed at the panel level. Even if new facts arise between the time of the panel and the appeal, the Appellate Body will refuse to look at them, as it did when Canada tried to get the US to submit new material regarding import levels in a dispute relating to softwood lumber. The absence of factual considerations is one of the reasons that panel reports tend to be more voluminous than those of the Appellate Body. The distinction between law and fact isn't always an easy one, and indeed the Appellate Body has decided that the application of a specific legal rule to a fact is itself a question of law that falls within the Appellate Body's sphere of competence. So, as we saw in the previous chapter, the Appellate Body is able to assess the legal concept of 'likeness' for the purposes of the national treatment test even where this requires them to look at how a particular product looks or tastes. Generally speaking, the Appellate Body will not interfere lightly with a panel's decision – it will only review determinations made by the panel where it has failed to make an objective assessment of the matter. The appeals tribunal won't 'second-guess' the panel in appreciating the significance of the facts that come before it, it will only correct an error in the panel's understanding of one of the WTO's rules as applied to those facts.

A key aspect of how judicial procedures unfold is establishing which party (the country bringing the complaint or the country responding to the complaint) bears the burden of proof, meaning that they have the onus of establishing whether or not something is the way they claim it to be. We are familiar with the phrase 'innocent until proven guilty', which means that the state must show that there is evidence that the accused individual committed the crime; we do not presume guilt. WTO dispute settlement is unusual in that both parties in the dispute have the burden of proof at different points in the proceedings. The initial burden of proof lies on the party asserting the affirmative of a particular claim. So, if Europe claims that Argentina is charging more than its bound tariff on imported window glass, it is up to Europe to show that this is true. This is a big deal in any judicial proceeding, because it structures the way in which the entire case is brought, including what arguments are made and in what order, what evidence is used and how it is handled. This initial burden requires that there is a 'prima facie', meaning on its face or clearly evident, indication of a violation of one of the WTO's rules, like national treatment or most favoured nation under the GATT. Once this is done, the burden of proof shifts to the defending party, which has to counter the claimed inconsistency with the WTO – either by demonstrating that the violation did not occur or that there was a justification for it. Some of the key justifications for breaking WTO law will be discussed later on.

Parties generally have a high degree of control over how they argue their case before panels, with somewhat less over the appeals process because of its restriction to the particular issues that were raised in the appeal. Arguments and evidence are submitted in written form, and panels and the Appellate Body are able to request additional written information as required. Parties are under an obligation to provide the court with all of the information that is requested by it. Panels and Appellate Body members are free to ask questions to parties for clarification of issues during the oral hearing stage. This is somewhat different to the judicial processes in many countries where the judges say almost nothing, simply allowing the parties to question each other. The purpose of the oral hearing is to provide the participating parties with the opportunity to present and argue their case in order to clarify the issues.

When rendering their decisions, panels and the Appellate Body must of course refer to the laws contained in the WTO agreements, like the GATT, because these are the basis upon which legal claims are made. Other sources of law that the WTO court may rely upon include other international treaties, particularly if both countries are party to them, as well as previous decisions of other panels and the Appellate Body. While there is no strict doctrine of precedent as exists under the Common Law of countries like the UK and the US, tribunals of the WTO are encouraged to follow previously adopted panel and Appellate Body reports addressing the same issues because this practice fosters the development of a coherent body of jurisprudence. This in turn helps clarify member countries' rights and obligations, achieving the vital predictability that is one of the objectives of the dispute settlement system. In light of the value of consistency, it is quite common to see panels and Appellate Body divisions cite previous panel and especially Appellate Body (higher in the hierarchy) rulings as support for their decisions. The internal coherence of the dispute settlement system's judicial reasoning is why trade lawyers and law students tend to become familiar with some of the 'leading cases' of the WTO courts. This also explains why WTO law can be studied as a special discipline within international law. There is now a sizeable body of WTO law experts, many of whom teach and write academic articles on the subject, and some of whom have lucrative professional practices as well. Another key source of law used by the panels and the Appellate Body in deciding cases are the rules of interpretation of treaties that are established under international law and enshrined in the Vienna Convention on the Law of Treaties. These principles, which essentially convey the need to interpret words according to their ordinary meaning, supplemented by the context in which they appear in a given treaty, are helpful in discerning the intention and purpose of words in the text of the various WTO treaties. Ambiguities over what certain words mean – such as 'likeness', 'benefit' or 'injury' – can make the difference between winning or losing a case, sometimes worth several millions if not billions of dollars to the parties involved.

Panellists and Appellate Body members are experts in WTO law, so they are not necessarily equipped with a sophisticated understanding of particular industries or complex scientific or even economic concepts. This is why the WTO courts are able to consult experts to assist them in rendering their decisions. WTO judges have the authority to seek information and technical advice from any individual or body they deem appropriate. This expert advice has been used in a number of cases. For example, a panel sought assistance from scientists regarding alleged risks associated with fresh, chilled and frozen salmon that had not been quarantined according to specific requirements imposed by the Australian government, which Australia had used to impose a ban on salmon imported from Canada. In that case, none of the experts consulted could find any scientific health-related justification for Australia's salmon regulations. Experts are normally chosen in consultation with both parties, not in a partisan way as in many domestic legal systems. Of course, experts cannot make the case for one of the parties.

In addition to conferring with individual experts, the WTO panels and Appellate Body may also seek assistance from specialized international organizations such as the World Health Organization, the World Intellectual Property Organization and the IMF. The WTO is expected to cooperate with each of these organizations in fulfilling its mandate, especially with the IMF, which establishes stable monetary exchange rates, because of the important role that currency manipulation can play in the distortion of the price of goods that are traded internationally.

Accessibility

The WTO's dispute settlement system is for members only – meaning that only the countries that are members of the WTO can use it. Private companies cannot bring claims through the system, nor can individuals or groups. It is often said that there is significant *indirect* access for trading companies, through the lobby efforts brought upon their own governments. I mentioned in the previous chapter that the bananas dispute was instigated in large part at the behest of Chiquita, the US banana company. The aircraft subsidies case was the consequence of complaints made by Boeing and Airbus to the US and EU governments respectively.

The importance of background political lobbying to the WTO dispute settlement process should not be understated. Indeed, one of the chief weaknesses of the WTO dispute settlement system is that it is often the disproportionate power of dominant industry groups which ultimately dictates the nature of the disputes that come before the WTO court, rather than those which affect the legitimate interests of citizens. While in theory the governments of the member states of the WTO should be quite willing to launch disputes against other states whenever a violation of one of the WTO trade promises is causing some harm to its domestic economy, but this is not always the case. The process of dispute settlement at the WTO can be expensive and is not always worth it where there aren't significant political as well as economic advantages at home. When a government responds to a complaint from a powerful firm, this gives the impression that the government takes that particular industry seriously and is willing to fight for it. This can translate to millions in donations as well as victory at the ballot box. Similarly, appealing unfavourable panel rulings offers vital political 'face-saving', showing that the government is doing everything it can to defend its own corporate citizens. Threatening to sue another country through the WTO court (as a number of Western countries have done recently in relation to China, for example) is sound vote-winning chest-thumping for politicians around the world. At the same time, powerless or disorganized citizen groups tend to have very little say in what complaints are brought or the resources that are deployed to defend them.

The ability of individuals or less well-organized groups like consumers to take part in the WTO dispute settlement process is almost non-existent. Not only do these groups lack the official standing needed to appear before the panels and Appellate Body, they don't wield the influence to get their governments to represent their interests. In that sense it is often said that the WTO court system suffers from inaccessibility, which is problematic given its importance to the livelihoods of many millions of people. The lack of access to the WTO dispute settlement system is further compounded by the fact that its hearings are confidential – they are not open to the public like most judicial systems are, at least in the developed world. In theory, if you want to watch a hearing at the US or UK supreme courts, you can, if you get to the courthouse early enough and are prepared to line up for an hour and go through the metal detectors. Some countries, like Canada, even televise the hearings of their supreme court. This is not the case with the WTO panels or appeals hearings. They take place effectively in secret at the WTO headquarters and never appear on TV.

The confidentiality of the WTO dispute settlement process is controversial because of the public nature of the matters being discussed. While the disputes indirectly affect private suppliers and traders as well as consumers, they are fundamentally about laws enacted by democratically elected governments. Therefore, we might expect that the evaluation of these decisions made under international law through the WTO courts should be open to public scrutiny, particularly where an issue relating to the broader public interest is at play.

Members of the public and other interested parties have a limited capacity to participate in the WTO dispute settlement process through the amicus curiae procedure. Amicus curiae or 'friend of the court' involvement in disputes is derived from the panel and Appellate Body's authority to accept and consider written briefs submitted by individuals, companies and organizations in order to assist them in making an objective assessment of the matter before them. This means that an organization can submit material to the court outlining how the outcome of the decision will affect them and why the judges should rule in a certain way. Participation by non-parties of this kind has been severely criticized by WTO members, primarily because it jeopardizes both the confidentiality and the efficiency of the dispute settlement process. This type of external involvement can interfere with the strict time frames of the dispute settlement process.

The Appellate Body attempted to clarify the rules on the acceptance of amicus curiae briefs in a 1998 dispute brought against the EU in relation to its ban on the material asbestos. Canada had challenged the EU's law on the basis that it lacked scientific proof of a risk to health. There were a significant number of non-parties including industry groups interested in taking part in the appeal (because of the health controversies surrounding various forms of asbestos), so the Appellate Body decided to set up procedural requirements that needed to be met by any person or entity wishing to file a written brief in the dispute. The court clarified that individuals and groups do not have the right to submit documents to the panels or Appellate Body – the decision to accept them rests with the discretion of the tribunals. One of the key requirements stipulated by the Appellate Body in the asbestos dispute was that there was a maximum page limit of twenty pages from each applicant or group. Eleven groups, including several NGOs, ended up submitting applications for amicus curiae status in the asbestos dispute, and the Appellate Body refused all of them on the basis of their failure to comply with their designated rules, a result that delighted many within the WTO community eager to preserve the traditional system. The amicus curiae issue remains quite contentious and there are as yet no official rules on the accepting of amicus briefs that are applicable to all disputes. To date there have been amicus curiae briefs submitted in sixteen Appellate Body proceedings, but so far in none of these instances did the tribunal decide that it was useful actually to consider the brief. This is somewhat worrisome given the WTO's need to cultivate an image of openness and transparency as an institution of global governance. Experiments in making the dispute settlement process more open, including inviting the public to watch hearings at the WTO headquarters in Geneva and streaming disputes online, have met with limited success. Since very few people actually took advantage of these facilities, it may be that perceived rather than actual access is the key.

Enforcement

Once a ruling is issued by a panel or Appellate Body and it is accepted by the WTO (which as we know is done automatically unless there is consensus not to), this entails legal consequences for the parties. This is why parties bring claims − if there wasn't some form of sanction for losing a case then there would be no point, other than possibly a moral one, in making an issue out of it in the first place. When the dispute settlement system determines that a country has violated a WTO agreement, that losing country must change its behaviour. It has to stop breaking the law. The country doesn't have to pay monetary compensation (or damages, as they are called in most domestic legal systems); it just has to stop misbehaving. The state must modify its laws so that they conform to its obligations under the terms of membership of the WTO. This is why it is sometimes said that WTO remedies are 'forward-looking' − they don't so much compensate injured member countries for what harm they suffered in the past, but simply ensure that the same injury doesn't happen again.

The system's lack of monetary remedies − compensating injured members for having their WTO rights violated − has been criticized by a number of commentators. In particular it is thought that giving cash to the country that has won a dispute could be more helpful to it than facilitating future trading opportunities, especially if the breach itself led to significant gains for the country losing the dispute. But the logic of the WTO places primacy on the fulfilment of one's obligations as a member, meaning preserving the access to foreign markets on a non-discriminatory basis. Allowing a country to reject that premise simply because it is able to pay is quite rightly seen as undermining the spirit of equality that embodies the WTO as an organization committed to liberalizing trade. A similar rationale might be applied to celebrities who commit crimes and who are forced to serve jail time. For someone with virtually inexhaustible wealth, a fine is simply not enough of a deterrent.

But what if the losing country does not change its laws to bring them into conformity with WTO law, as determined by the dispute settlement system? What are the consequences of not obeying the rules? A country can't be thrown in jail, and as there are no monetary damages, they can't be fined either. The WTO certainly cannot (and would not) sanction military invasion because of a breach of international trade law. We are far too civilized for that sort of thing in the twenty-first century, particularly since one of the purposes of the original GATT, signed after World War II, was to maintain peace.

If the dispute settlement system decides that a country has done something wrong, it must bring its laws into conformity with its WTO obligations, re-establishing the benefits that are engendered by membership of the organization. If it does not do this within a reasonable time (the length of which is itself subject to assessment under the dispute settlement system and is usually less than a few months) the offending member state should offer compensation or, as an alternative, suffer some kind of penalty that is itself economically harmful. The disputing states will enter into negotiations to determine a mutually acceptable type and degree of compensation, such as deeper tariff reductions in areas of particular interest to the winning complainant. Compensation is actually quite rare in WTO dispute settlement. In the case involving Japanese tax rates on the alcoholic drink shochu, the parties were able to agree on temporary additional trade conces-sions for other products of interest to the US and the EU.

If no satisfactory compensation is agreed between the two parties, the complaining side may ask the WTO for permission to impose limited trade sanctions, which are framed as suspen-sions of trade concessions that the losing member enjoyed by virtue of its membership of the WTO. Such sanctions, which are effective tariffs levied against the losing country by the winning country, are seen as a preferable alternative to unilateral retali-ation by the winning member, which may be excessive and also have an air of hostility or aggression. By having the response authorized centrally through the WTO itself, the consequences of a breach of WTO law are both neutral and measured. This multilateral punishment (although the WTO would never use that word) also carries the gravitas of condemnation by the inter-national community. This can itself act as an additional deterrent because of the effect that this has on the reputation of the coun-try that has been found to be in breach of international law. The authorized sanctions, sometimes referred to as retaliation, should be imposed in the same sector as the dispute, meaning that you should not increase tariffs on machinery for a dispute relating to textiles. But, if this is not practical or would not be effective, the winning party can suspend trade concessions in other sectors, a particularly potent weapon known as 'cross-retaliation'. Cross-retaliation has been authorized by the WTO only a handful of times. In allowing this remedy the objective is to minimize the risk that the dispute will spread into other sectors, worsening the already damaged trade relations.

The key limitation is that the retaliation, in whatever sector, must be equivalent to the injury sustained by the winning complainant country. It cannot be more. The purpose of retali-ation measures is not punishment; nor, strictly speaking, is it deterrence. It is simply to restore the equilibrium so that func-tional, open trade relations can continue.

CROSS-RETALIATION AND INTELLECTUAL PROPERTY RIGHTS

One of the most extreme cases of authorized cross-retaliation arose in relation to a dispute in which the island country of Antigua won a case at the WTO against the US about cross-border gambling services. The US had outlawed Internet-based gambling websites operated out of Antigua in violation of its commitments under the General Agreement on Trade in Services (GATS). The US had attempted to argue that it was legally allowed to prevent these websites from operating in the US because they were a risk to its 'public morals'. This defence, although in theory valid under WTO law, was rejected by the panel and Appellate Body and the US was ordered to change its laws. But the US never did this, prompting Antigua to ask for compensation totalling US $21 million per year. The rationale for this request was that retaliation under WTO rules doesn't always help a little country. In fact, retaliating against a giant like the US by suspending trade concessions could do more trade damage to Antigua. Instead, Antigua was allowed, in early 2013, to suspend concessions up to this value under the Trade Related Aspects of Intellectual Property Rights (TRIPS) Agreement. This means that the WTO authorized Antigua to allow pirate websites selling reproductions of US DVDs and CDs. Antigua continues to threaten to set up a state-sponsored piracy website as payback for the gambling dispute. It is likely that these threats are merely intended to encourage the US to pay Antigua the cash equivalent of the retaliation. The effectiveness of this strategy may depend on the political clout of Hollywood as well as artists' organizations. Of course, while it may be legal for the Antiguans to allow such websites to operate from within their territory, it is still quite likely that a US citizen using such a website could be prosecuted under US domestic law for violating copyright rules.

The WTO's system of enforcement for violation of its agreements has been condemned for lacking teeth. It is often said that there is no truly effective sanction for countries that do not comply with dispute settlement rulings. Retaliation, it is often argued, is only effective when it is used by a country of relatively equal economic power to the losing party; otherwise it is an empty threat that is ultimately self-defeating for the winning country that imposes it. It is particularly unhelpful for developing countries where the suspension of trade concessions would be barely noticed by a large, developed country. More creative types of retaliation, for example under the intellectual property agreement, or conventional monetary payments, could offer a solution.

It's important that people recognize that overall, the record of compliance with WTO panel and Appellate Body recommendations is quite good, although far from perfect. About one quarter of disputes result in some form of non-compliance, whether it is failure to implement fully the required changes to the law or taking too long to do so. Of course, no justice system can ever expect to achieve full compliance – check out how many debt collection agencies there are in your area, not to mention bailiffs. Given the complexities of the legal obligations and the myriad social and economic implications of international trade relations within the global community, the WTO dispute settlement system has done very well. It is truly a remarkable achievement in international law.

4

Playing fair: non-tariff barriers to trade

The GATT, and the WTO after it, were immensely successful in reducing tariffs, which had been the chief barrier to trade in the twentieth century. But the attachment in many countries to protectionism – safeguarding the interests of the domestic economy, meaning firms and workers – remained. Structuring laws to favour local over foreign goods is probably as politically important in the twenty-first century as it has ever been, despite the widespread endorsement of free trade ideology by economists, diplomats and policymakers the world over.

The success of tariff negotiations, coupled with the non-discrimination guarantees of most favoured nation and national treatment, accordingly led to new challenges for politicians who wanted to help their own producers. The WTO's increasing membership sought creative ways to favour their own goods, in conjunction with sticking to GATT rules on tariff bindings and agnosticism with respect to a product's origin. In particular, the unfair trade practices of subsidization and dumping have now become the most readily used weapons in the arsenal of the trade protectionist. Recognizing the danger of these key policy tools, the WTO realized that it needed to expand its mandate to address these types of trade-distorting practices. Drafted in the 1940s, the GATT rules on subsidies and dumping were inadequate for the modern era, so the WTO created two dedicated agreements to address these highly popular and contentious fields of national economic policy. We will look at both of them in this chapter.

Subsidization

If you cannot make foreign products more expensive because tariffs have been essentially eliminated, then why not make domestic ones cheaper? As long as the local product is less expensive than the equivalent foreign one, it doesn't matter how this is achieved, at least from the perspective of protecting your own producers. This strategy – helping domestic firms keep their costs low so that they can make their products cheaper – is known as subsidization.

Assistance granted by national governments to make certain sectors or companies more competitive than they are in reality operates as a market distortion. In that sense, it is as bad as a tariff. In some ways it is even worse because, unlike a tariff, a subsidy does not generate revenue for the government, it actually consumes it. This is one of the reasons that economists tend to agree that subsidies are generally inefficient and should not be used as tools of economic policy. Yet their use persists throughout the world. One possible justification for the use of subsidies is that they generate so-called 'positive externalities', meaning additional beneficial consequences beyond simply helping the target company or industry, many of which can be difficult to quantify. These can include increased employment, regional regeneration and improvements to the general social welfare. Some of these may not have any trade-distortive effects.

Of course, resistance to government assistance in the economy can be seen as a liberal Western, market-oriented conception of what constitutes the proper sphere of governmental involvement. Countries with a tradition of governmental supervision of the economy, such as that practised by the countries of the former Soviet Union, as well as (to a degree) China today, may not see anything wrong with what we would call subsidization. Indeed, there are a number of very significant state-owned enterprises in Russia and China, as well as in Latin America, where there is a similarly strong tradition of state interventionism in the economy. Companies get help from governments all the time in these places. In fact, involvement in commercial activities is very much what governments do. Where there is no clear demarcation between the government and the private entity, it is very difficult to ascertain whether or not a subsidy can be said to exist.

The Agreement on Subsidies and Countervailing Measures

The aim of the Agreement on Subsidies and Countervailing Measures (SCM), which was enacted along with the creation of the WTO in 1995, was to clarify and improve the limited GATT rules on subsidies. The SCM controls the extent to which countries can take action to counter the effects of subsidies that have been used by other members. WTO members can use the WTO dispute settlement system, as outlined in the previous chapter, in order to get another country to withdraw the subsidy or to remove its adverse effects. Countries are also empowered to launch their own investigation and ultimately charge an extra fee, which is known as a 'countervailing duty' or 'countervailing measure', on subsidies that are found to be harming domestic producers.

One of the most important features of the SCM is that it contains a definition of subsidy. According to the agreement, a subsidy is a financial contribution by a government that confers a benefit to an entity in its territory. This will include things like direct transfers of money, such as grants or loans, or when governmental revenue that is otherwise due (like income tax) is forgone or not collected. It can also include situations where governments provide goods or services, like dedicated roads or the supply of utilities to particular companies, or even where a government buys goods from a company. So, in short, there are many types of governmental activities that can fall under the definition of subsidy and in theory attract the attention of the WTO.

The scope of the concept of subsidy was illustrated in one of the most enduring trade disputes between Canada and the US involving softwood lumber, the type of wood often used as a building material in houses. The US brought a claim at the WTO based on the assertion that the Canadian lumber industry enjoyed a subsidy from the provincial governments of Canada (primarily British Columbia) giving Canadian companies an unfair advantage over American ones. This subsidy took the form of a price paid to lumber companies by British Columbia for each tree, called a 'stumpage fee', set by the government as the owner of the trees. Crucially, this was not a natural market price per tree as in the US, where trees are predominately owned privately. In Canada, the lumber companies were effectively being supplied with trees by the government at set prices that were below the market rate. In determining that this benefit received by the Canadian companies should be considered a subsidy, the WTO Appellate Body concluded that the range of governmental measures that can be considered subsidies and therefore fall within the sphere of SCM, such as this type of 'price support', is quite broad.

Of course, the concept of government can itself be problematic, especially in situations where the state plays a larger role in the economy than we are used to in the West. This issue is further complicated by the many different levels of government found in most developed countries, including national, regional and local. The difficulty in coming to grips with the concept of a 'public body', which is a phrase that also appears in the SCM when referencing the source of a subsidy, was highlighted in a dispute between the US and China regarding various attempts by the US to counter Chinese subsidization in a number of industries including steel and rubber. China had argued that contributions made by Chinese state-owned enterprises to private companies were not benefits and therefore not subsidies. The Appellate Body ultimately agreed with China, ruling that in order to be considered a public body and therefore capable of subsidizing, that entity must perform governmental functions and have the authority to give commands to a private body. This determination would need to be done on a case-by-case basis. On an examination of the relevant companies providing the contribution, the Chinese state-owned enterprise did not have these powers, so the assistance that it offered could not be deemed a subsidy.

The concept of benefit is also contentious, but it is clear that it encapsulates that which is received by the recipient company and not that which is given by the government. This distinction becomes important when the WTO panels and Appellate Body have to assess the quantity of the subsidy for the purposes of sanctioning a response from the complaining country. The idea is that the recipient has been made better off than it would otherwise have been in the absence of that contribution from the government. One way of identifying this type of situation is where the government provides goods or services to the company but the company either does not pay for them, or pays an amount that is below the prevailing market price for those goods or services in the country in question. Obviously this is the type of thing that is going to require a significant amount of evidence, much of which will be presented with the help of economists and other specialists.

AIRBUS AND BOEING

The US aeronautics company Boeing had been the dominant manu-facturer of large civil aircraft until the European Airbus came along in the early 1970s, specifically with a view to competing with the American giant. By the late 1990s, Airbus had become the major player in this niche industry and seemed to be gaining ground on its rival every year. The stakes were raised further when each company invested billions in the research and development of new jumbo aircraft designs, ultimately becoming Airbus's massive A380 and, a few years later, Boeing's futuristic Dreamliner. But things weren't quite what they seemed. Both sides felt that the other was playing dirty by getting help from its government in the form of subsidiza-tion. In 2004, at the prompting of Boeing (a major source of political donations), the US initiated a dispute against Europe at the WTO, alleging that the EU was subsidizing Airbus in violation of the SCM. The EU fired back, claiming that the US government was doing the same thing for Boeing. At the time, the Boeing–Airbus dispute was believed to be the most expensive case ever heard before the WTO court. The dispute was fought intensely over several years, with an appeal as well as additional procedural hearings on compliance. Like a split decision in a boxing match, each party claimed victory as the WTO ruled that both Airbus and Boeing had been receiving billions of dollars of subsidies from their respective governments over decades. Boeing had enjoyed more than US $4 billion in illegal subsidies for research and development assistance, much of which had been in the form of access to facilities as well as equipment and employees that were provided under the NASA contracts with the US Department of Defense. Airbus meanwhile had benefited from US $18 billion in state aid loans, which although legal, because they were repayable to the government, led to more than three hundred lost aircraft sales for Boeing. The issue remains partially unresolved because it is not yet clear how each government is going to follow through with the rulings issued by the Appellate Body, and it seems as though some of the governmental assistance by both the US and the EU will continue until a clear agreement on compliance has been reached, a situation which itself raises the spectre of retali-ation through trade sanctions. It is possible that the ongoing nego-tiations for the Transatlantic Trade and Investment Partnership (a comprehensive free trade and investment treaty between the US and the EU) could become the forum through which the Boeing–Airbus battle is ultimately resolved.

Since the concept of benefit from government is so wide that it could cover all sorts of governmental involvement with the private sector, the SCM relies on the concept of specificity to delimit the kind of governmental assistance that falls within the WTO's concern over market distortions. A specific subsidy is one that is available only to an enterprise, industry or group of enterprises in the country that grants the subsidy. Only these types of subsidies are within the sphere of the SCM. Other, general or non-specific subsidies, meaning ones which are widely available within a given economy, are deemed not to be problematic from a standpoint of market distortion. This limitation legitimizes many of the general schemes of governmental assistance adopted around the world in order to deal with issues like unemployment, underdevelopment or the effects of recessions. Accordingly grants for research and development, student loan support for higher education and general infrastructure projects, such as roads and bridges for use by all, do not constitute SCM illegal subsidies. Furthermore, there is no specificity if the government sets out neutral objective criteria governing the eligibility for the subsidy which does not favour certain firms over other ones, meaning there is no bias or favouritism. In the dispute between the US and China over alleged subsidies to steel and rubber industries, the Appellate Body clarified that the concept of specificity is also a flexible one and its determination will be done on a case-by-case basis (more discretion to the WTO courts), but that specificity will be established if there is a clear restriction on the particular enterprise or industry to which the contribution will apply.

There are two types of subsidies that are subject to control by the SCM: prohibited and actionable. Prohibited subsidies, often described as 'red light' subsidies under a traffic light system of categorization, are those that require recipients to meet certain export targets or to use domestic instead of imported goods. These subsidies are prohibited because they are intentionally designed by the governments that use them to distort international trade

– they are clear weapons of protectionism aimed at making local goods artificially more competitive. In 1999, Australia was found to have violated the SCM by subsidizing a company that produced leather for car seats. The financial assistance offered by the government to the leather company in the form of grants fell into the prohibited category because it was clearly aimed at helping increasing exports to an implied target set by the government. The WTO panel inferred this from the fact that the Australian government knew that its domestic market was too small to absorb all of the automotive leather being produced. There just weren't enough cars in Australia to justify the production of that many leather seats, so the assistance must have been intended to encourage sales abroad.

Actionable or 'yellow light' subsidies require that the complaining country demonstrates that the subsidy has had an adverse effect on its interests. If this cannot be shown, then the subsidy is permitted. On the traffic light analogy, you can go through a yellow light if it is unsafe to stop – perhaps the only instance where my previous background as a traffic prosecutor linked to my work in world trade law. Three types of harm are defined under the SCM: one country's subsidies can hurt a domestic industry in an importing country; they can hurt rival exporters from another country when the two exporters compete in third markets; and domestic subsidies in one country can hurt exporters that are trying to compete in the subsidizing country's domestic market, even if they have not done so yet. In a dispute regarding South Korea's alleged subsidization of computer chips (dynamic random access memory) the WTO panel was required to assess whether the assistance granted by South Korea to various companies which had not been clearly export motivated had actually caused any injury to Japanese firms in the same industry. The panel considered other possible causes of the harm to the Japanese random access memory chip industry, including reduced demand and changed habits of consumption for those products as well as developments in technology, both of which had themselves caused the sales of Japanese firms to decline. Demonstrating the harmful effect of a subsidy can require a lot of evidence.

If it is determined by the WTO dispute settlement process that a prohibited subsidy exists, it must be withdrawn immediately. If it is not, the complaining party can take countermeasures. If domestic producers in the complaining country are injured by imports of subsidized products, then countervailing duties can be imposed. And if a panel or the Appellate Body rules that an actionable subsidy does have an adverse effect, the subsidy must be withdrawn or its adverse effect must be removed. As with prohibited subsidies, if this is not done, the complaining country can impose a countervailing duty to counter the damaging effects on its domestic industry.

The countervailing measure response can only be imposed by the winning country after that country has conducted an extensive investigation of the subsidy and the damaging effects it has caused. There are quite sophisticated rules detailing whether a product has been subsidized, criteria for determining whether imports of subsidized products are hurting a domestic industry, rules on how to initiate and conduct the investigations and finally on how to implement the countermeasures and for what duration. The subsidized exporter, meaning the private company benefiting from assistance from its home country, can also agree to raise its export prices, instead of it being charged the countervailing duty, as a form of settlement or compromise in order to escape the wrath of retaliation.

A more creative remedy was implemented by the WTO in the dispute, mentioned above, relating to Australia's subsidy of automotive leather. It was determined in that case that simply requiring Australia to stop helping its major leather producer was not enough, because this firm had already been given a significant advantage by virtue of the grants. So the WTO courts ordered the

Australian automotive leather company to pay back the subsidy to the government, effectively fining them. While the WTO cannot impose conditions on companies directly – it only deals with countries – it insisted that Australia collect the money from the company, meaning that a refusal by the company to comply would have resulted in a breach of Australian domestic law. This backward-looking monetary remedy is highly unusual for the WTO and it has not yet been used again. The WTO court justified this response by explaining that the money had already been used by the company to produce new inventory, so although it was in a sense punishment for past behaviour, the effects, namely increased exports, were yet to take effect.

The importance of subsidies to the economies of developing countries can be immense. Many vital industries would not survive without them because they cannot compete internationally, in particular with exporters from the developed world. As a consequence, the least developed countries, meaning those with less than US $1000 per capita GDP, are exempted from all of the WTO's rules on prohibited export subsidies. Other developing countries were given until 2003 to get rid of their export subsidies, with countries newly joining the WTO given time to phase out their subsidy regimes. Because subsidies can play a crucial role in countries that are making the transition from command economies to market-based ones, these countries are also exempt from some of the requirements imposed by the SCM.

As I mentioned earlier in this book, one of the most contentious areas of subsidies, and indeed of the WTO in its entirety, relates to agriculture. The prevalence of subsidies in agriculture is in no small part because of the political clout of farming groups around the world, in particular the US and Europe, as well as the importance of subsistence agriculture to millions of people in the developing world. Trade in agricultural products, which falls outside the GATT regime (because the powerful negotiating countries of the developed world did not have a competitive advantage in this sector that they wanted to protect), has become highly distorted because of export subsidies which would not have been allowed for industrial products. Indeed it is often asserted that the EU and the US's assistance to domestic farming has done more damage to the weak economies of Africa than could possibly be remedied by the billions in aid given supposedly to eradicate poverty in these countries. This is perhaps the WTO's greatest failure and a clear instance of its uneven treatment of rich and poor countries.

A special agricultural agreement was created at the time of the WTO's inception in 1995 in order to control this type of highly sensitive subsidization. The Agreement on Agriculture allows countries to support their rural economies, distinguishing between support programmes that stimulate production directly, which must be cut back, and those that are considered to have no direct trade effect, which are allowed. Gradual reductions in agricultural subsidies have been imposed on several new WTO members as conditions of their accession. When Russia joined the WTO in 2012 it was allowed to use agricultural subsidies of US \$9 billion, but this amount was required to fall to US \$4.4 billion by 2018. It also promised to forgo completely export-oriented subsidies in agriculture. Negotiations on eliminating agricultural subsidies have been one of the sticking points in the Doha Round negotiations and there remains much to be achieved in removing distortions in this area. The EU still spends over thirty billion euros per year on agricultural subsidies, a significant portion of its annual budget. US farm subsidies are of a similar size and this is unlikely to change any time soon. These figures are shocking when one considers that many of the beneficiaries of these handouts are not small family farms but large agribusinesses and wealthy landowners. Agricultural subsidies are quite rightly described as a transfer from the poor to the rich.

Finally, you may be wondering, given that the WTO has a tight regime of control over governmental assistance to the private sector, how the multi-billion-dollar bailouts of the banks and car companies associated with the 2008–09 recession could possibly have been allowed. Was the help given to car companies like General Motors, insurers like AIG, and banks like the Royal Bank of Scotland in the aftermath of the financial crisis illegal subsidization? Probably. It was clearly assistance from a government that conferred a benefit to specific enterprises, although there may have been a general economic need rather than an export-oriented purpose. Whether it caused injury to other industries is debatable, but a link could likely be proven, at least in some instances. So why did no one bring this type of case through the WTO courts? The simplest answer is that everyone was doing it. The EU, the US, Japan, in fact almost all the major economies, had some form of bailout programme during the darkest days of the crisis. So, if one country had brought a claim, others would have shot back and the result would have been a bloodbath. The WTO was never meant to deal directly with the fallout from a worldwide financial crisis, although one of the GATT's initial purposes was to prevent another Great Depression–like scenario through escalating protectionism.

Dumping

Another tool of unfair trade intended to address the declining availability of tariffs is dumping. Dumping is the practice in which goods are sold at below their cost of production to eradicate competition in foreign markets. This strategy seems counter-intuitive at first (why would you sell something at a loss?), but becomes clear when it is recognized that companies are willing to suffer initial losses in order to take control of a market over the long term. In terms of its role in international trade, dumping takes the form of selling in the foreign market at a price lower than the price in the home market. Again this seems ridiculous at first glance. Surely you should charge more overseas than you do right next door to the factory where something is made? But you may be quite willing to charge less abroad because you want to gain control of that foreign market, removing the local competition in the long term. Asserting market dominance may be best described as a marathon, not a sprint.

Economists consider this practice to be anti-competitive behaviour that ultimately leads to damaging market distortions. Once the foreign supplier gains control of the market by destroying the local competition, it is then free to act as a monopolist, charging excessive prices that deprive consumers of choice. Dumping is now one of the chief modern barriers to free trade, and there are believed to be a number of ongoing incidences, especially by firms in China as well as Russia. Recent high-profile examples include the alleged dumping of solar panels exported by China into Europe and Russian steel products also into Europe.

The Anti-Dumping Agreement

As with the SCM, the WTO's Anti-Dumping Agreement was intended to elaborate upon the very basic rules on dumping contained in the old GATT. The WTO's Anti-Dumping Agreement doesn't govern dumping itself, but the potential response to it, namely anti-dumping duties. It must be remembered that the WTO has no power to censure private companies which dump their products into other countries. But it can regulate the way that the importing country reacts to dumping by levying extra fees on those products.

If the country of origin feels that anti-dumping actions taken by the importing country were excessive or inappropriate (anti-dumping duties that were charged were too high or should not have been charged at all), then the WTO can punish that importing country. This is because an anti-dumping duty charged in response to dumping allows that country to act in a way that would normally break the GATT rules on tariff bindings and non-discrimination among trading partners. An anti-dumping duty is a charge beyond the level of the committed tariff rate on a given product, and it is only levied on products from that particular country from which the dumped goods originate. This extra fee is meant to bring the price of that good closer to the 'normal value' of the product (the price that it really should have been sold at) or to remove the injury to the domestic industry in the importing country.

One of the great difficulties with regulating anti-dumping is that there are many different ways of calculating whether a particular product is being dumped and by how much. Is it really fair to nail a supplier with an anti-dumping charge, or is the difference in the price of the good so small that it doesn't really matter? Is the price being charged really lower than it should be? Or, put another way, does the good appear more competitive than it really is?

The Anti-Dumping Agreement provides three ways to calculate a product's 'normal value' – the main one based on the product's price in the exporter's home market. In a dispute brought against the US in 1998 for the anti-dumping duties it imposed on hot-rolled steel (sheets of steel unwound off giant drums) originating from Europe, the WTO courts decided that in arriving at the 'normal value' of a product the sale must be in the ordinary course of business (meaning not a one-off or bulk sale or one made to a friend), the product must be for consumption in the exporting country and of course the comparison must be between 'like products'. Under the Anti-Dumping Agreement, 'likeness' is said to mean identical, or alike in all respects, a somewhat narrower view than we saw under GATT. Differences that might affect price comparability, such as those reflecting the conditions of sale, should be discounted. For example, in an anti-dumping case brought against the US by South Korea relating to stainless steel, the WTO court considered whether it should discount differences in prices that were paid by certain local purchasers because of a recent bankruptcy (when they were desperate to sell), ultimately deciding that these were irrelevant in establishing the normal price because the bankruptcy and the ensuing lower prices were unanticipated by the supplier.

If information regarding the product's price in the home market is not available, maybe because there are not enough sales at home or the price at home is itself artificial because it is set by the government (as in a command economy), the price charged by the exporter in a third country can be used. Alternatively, a 'constructed cost' can be used, which is a price based on a combination of the exporter's production costs, other reasonable administrative expenses and normal profit margins. As you can imagine, establishing these sorts of prices can be quite technical and require extensive evidence.

Anti-dumping duties are only allowed if the lower price of the good in the export market is hurting industry there. In order to demonstrate this, a detailed investigation is required which must be conducted according to requirements set out in the Anti-Dumping Agreement. Investigations are conducted by the government of the importing country but they must conform to WTO rules, which demand that all relevant economic factors that could have affected the industry in question are considered. This means that you can't allege that an industry has been hurt by dumping if the industry is simply uncompetitive, for example because it pays wages that are too high or makes products that nobody wants. In addition to rules about the type of evidence that can be tendered during the investigation, the WTO also requires that the importing country give all interested parties the opportunity to present their case, essentially allowing them to explain that they have not dumped goods or, if they have, that they are prepared to raise the price to an agreed level in order to avoid the anti-dumping duty. Anti-dumping investigations have to end if it turns out that the margin of dumping is so small that it is insignificant (less than two percent of the export price of the product) or if the volume of the dumped imports is also negligible (if the volume of dumped imports from one country is less than three percent of the total imports of that product).

CHINESE SOLAR PANELS

In response to the rising cost of electricity and concerns about overuse of fossil fuel, solar panels have become a popular source of heating for homes and commercial buildings. Photovoltaic cells in the panels convert sunlight into electricity, saving potentially hundreds of dollars per year as well as tonnes of carbon dioxide emissions. Unfortunately solar panels are relatively expensive to build and install, which may explain why many millions of consumers in Europe choose to get their solar panels from where they can be produced at cheaper cost. As with many manufactured things in the twenty-first century, solar panels can be made cheaper in China. No problem there. In fact, many environmentalists were quite happy to offset the high initial costs of solar power by tapping into efficient Chinese manufacturing. But when solar panels from China were sold at a price below what they actually cost to make in Chinese factories, the European trading authorities got upset. In 2013, the EU decided to impose anti-dumping duties on solar panels imported from China, claiming that the underpriced panels had caused the loss of 25,000 jobs in the EU. The solar panel imports from China are worth well over US $20 billion, making this the largest anti-dumping case ever instigated by the EU. The EU raised the tariff rate on solar panels by almost twelve percent, causing many to fear that China would retaliate by imposing increased tariffs on a number of products it imports from Europe. Thankfully, the issue of the EU anti-dumping duties on Chinese solar panels never reached the stage of formal WTO dispute settlement; it was resolved through consultations in early 2014. The solar panel dumping matter was interesting because it placed the EU in a difficult position with respect to two of its key policies – free trade and environmental protection. Anti-dumping duties would send a clear message that Europe expects China to observe free trade by avoiding the anti-competitive use of dumping in order to corner the European market for a popular new product. But with higher tariffs imposed on Chinese solar panels, these important tools for offsetting climate change and reducing fossil fuel dependency would have become significantly more expensive, possibly even out of reach of the average European consumer. Of course, there is also the political value in teaching China a lesson – if China had been stung with anti-dumping duties on solar panels, it might have been discouraged from flooding the EU with all sorts of artificially cheap stuff, as some people believe it has done. More importantly, with the solar panel matter resolved for the time being, China now appears content not to bring its own dumping case against Europe with regard to overly cheap French and Italian wine.

One of the most contentious and highly technical issues in anti-dumping in recent years related to the practice of 'zeroing' in setting the margin of dumping for the purpose of setting an appropriate anti-dumping duty. Zeroing was a strategy used by the US when it calculated the level of anti-dumping duties that it imposed on a number of countries including Mexico, Europe, Ecuador and Japan. When establishing whether or not dumping of a particular product had occurred, and if so by how much, the US had been using price data from a number of countries in which the relevant good was sold, but it conveniently ignored situations where the price charged was higher (suggesting no dumping) rather than factoring this into the overall assessment of the product's normal price in other markets. This ploy, known as zeroing because it treated what was a negative margin (a higher price) as a zero instead of a negative number, has now been banned by the WTO.

A simple example may be helpful to illustrate this concept. Imagine that pencils made in Mongolia are being sold at $5 per box in Canada. The Canadian government is suspicious that these Mongolian pencils are being dumped, that is, sold at a price below their actual cost to the manufacturer in Mongolia. In order to succeed at the WTO on a claim of dumping, Canada has to prove that the pencils are being sold below cost, but there is no evidence available as to the normal price of pencils in Mongolia because the Mongolian pencil industry is a state-owned monopoly, so the prices charged to the home market are artificial. Instead, to construct an average normal price, the Canadian government looks at the price the Mongolian pencil suppliers are charging in a few other countries. The price in Argentina is $6 ($1 higher than in Canada). The price in South Africa is $7 ($2 higher than in Canada). But the price charged in Norway is only $2 ($3 *lower* than in Canada). When calculating the average price difference, Canada must add up the difference for the three countries. The calculations *should* be: $1+2+(-3)=0$. The overall average difference is 0, meaning that the world average is the same as Canada, so there doesn't appear to be any dumping. But Canada wants to find dumping of pencils so that it can impose anti-dumping duties on Mongolia. So instead it substitutes the negative value it found in Norway for a zero (0 instead of -3). With this shrewd calculation based on 'zeroing' the negative value then becomes: $1+2+\mathbf{0}=3$. By this method, the average world price comes out as $3 more than in Canada, indicating that the pencils in Canada are artificially cheap, suggesting dumping.

Without this practice of zeroing it is now harder to demonstrate that dumping has occurred, and when it has occurred, the legitimate level of anti-dumping duties should be lower. It is now clear in WTO law that, when comparing prices using a weighted average of prices in various different countries, the entirety of the prices for all comparable transactions involving the product must be considered during the dumping investigation and the calculation of the dumping margin.

It is worth noting that it is possible to apply anti-dumping duties on products where there is a threat of material injury to the domestic industry, without actual damage yet being demonstrated. In the softwood lumber dispute between the US and Canada (which was both a dumping case as well as a subsidy case – subsidies often enable companies to charge lower prices abroad) it was determined by the WTO court that further dumped imports were imminent and that unless protective action was taken, a material injury would occur in the near future. In assessing whether or not there has been dumping, the panels and Appellate Body will accordingly look at whether imports are entering the country that will significantly depress prices in that particular industry. They will also look at existing inventories of the allegedly dumped good.

In asserting that you are entitled to levy an anti-dumping duty, a causal link must also be established between the dumped good and the injury. This means again that other factors which have led to problems in the particular industry, not related to the lower-priced good from abroad, such as changes in consumer demand, improvements in technology or overpaid wages, must be discounted. This is called the 'non-attribution' requirement and was illustrated clearly in the hot-rolled steel case mentioned above. Allegations of dumping cannot be used to disguise a poorly performing industry, just as anti-dumping duties cannot be used as a shield against stronger competitors.

Lastly it should be noted that exporters or producers that have dumped products into a foreign market may try to get around anti-dumping duties that have been imposed on them, by changing the characteristics of the product so that it does not attract the higher tariff. So if an anti-dumping duty has been imposed on shirts, a supplier could add an extra button or lapel and then label the product a sweater (or jumper as the British say) in order to evade the charge. An exporter could also move part of its assembly or manufacturing operations to the importing country or even a third country, so that the good no longer technically originates from the country upon which the anti-dumping duties have been imposed. Whether or not these circumvention measures are allowed depends on the national laws of each WTO member; the WTO itself does not yet have any rules on these strategies.

Subsidies and dumping are now among the most popular tools of unfair trade being employed around the world. As tariffs continue to decline in usefulness as instruments of trade protectionism, there are poised to be many more negotiations involving the removal of subsidies at the WTO, just as there are likely to be many more impositions of anti-dumping duties that may be challenged through WTO dispute settlement. As we shall see, attempts to impede the free flow of traded goods can also take the form of what might appear to be quite legitimate non-trade and even non-economic public policy concerns.

5

Money isn't everything: public interest exceptions to WTO rules

It has often been said, especially by the anti-globalizationists, that the WTO is not sensitive enough to things other than international trade. In its single-minded pursuit of free trade among nations, so the argument goes, the WTO has ignored far too many important issues, like the environment, culture and human rights. These social policy objectives do not matter only to fringe protest groups, however. Very often, regulation in these areas is of vital interest to the broader citizenship of the member countries of the WTO, too. Problems can arise when laws that have been enacted to protect these important policy goals, like the environment or culture, come into conflict with a country's WTO obligations. Where a country has a legitimate non-trade policy, the WTO system may allow for such laws to be maintained, even where they violate tariff commitments and the non-discrimination guarantees.

Of course, it's not that simple. Just as countries eager to protect local industries are using creative strategies like subsidies and dumping instead of old-fashioned tariffs, they can also exploit the WTO's recognition of important non-trade matters as a disguised barrier to trade. In fact, it has often been suggested by some people in developing countries that rich countries pretend to respect things like the environment and human rights in their national laws at least partially as a way of strategically favouring their own products. Concepts like human rights protection or climate change mitigation might be viewed as the intellectual legacy of the decadent West, which has had centuries to consolidate its position of wealth, indulging in trivialities while the world's poor countries struggle to get their people out of poverty and establish basic standards of living.

A balance must be struck between fulfilling legitimate non-trade public policy objectives and maintaining WTO obligations of minimizing barriers to trade. This is done primarily through built-in exceptions for specific non-trade goals contained in the GATT, as well as special additional allowances for trade-related economic emergencies and national security. These highly controversial provisions of the WTO regime are the focus of this chapter. We'll start with an overview of GATT's celebrated (or notorious, depending on your point of view) General Exceptions.

The General Exceptions

The WTO does not have an environmental agreement – it is not an environmental agency – but it is clearly mindful of the potential environmental impacts of some of its policies. The WTO promises that its various rules on liberalizing trade should be interpreted in line with the objective of 'sustainable development'. This means economic advancement through international trade must contemplate the conservation of natural resources for future generations. Things should be both shared and replaced as they are used. This doesn't just mean things that have an obvious economic value, like trees for wood or fish to eat, or fossil fuels for our cars. It can also include exhaustible natural resources that are intrinsically valuable simply because they are alive and are at risk of depletion, like sea turtles.

In perhaps the most famous dispute that has ever come before the WTO courts, India, Malaysia, Pakistan and Thailand brought a joint complaint against the US for a ban it imposed on the importation of shrimp products. This was in 1997, only two years after the WTO was created. The basis of the US ban was the protection of sea turtles which were allegedly harmed during shrimp harvesting by companies from these Asian countries. The US had identified seven species of sea turtle which are found throughout the world in tropical and subtropical oceans. Under US law, five of these species found in US waters were considered endangered. As a consequence, the US required all US shrimp trawlers to use 'turtle exclusion devices' to prevent sea turtles from being killed accidentally during shrimp harvesting using giant nets dragged along behind the ships. Shrimp from countries that did not use these devices was banned. Although an import ban violates the GATT's prohibition on quotas, a provision of the GATT, the General Exceptions, allows for breach of this rule for purposes relating to 'the conservation of natural resources'. The US tried to use this exception to justify the ban and the four Asian countries complained.

The WTO Appellate Body ruled that countries have the right to enact laws to protect the environment, which can include the protection of endangered species like sea turtles. The language used at the beginning of the GATT established that the WTO members agreed that sustainable (meaning environmentally conscious) economic development was a goal of the trading system and should be taken into account as 'colour, texture and shading' in interpreting the agreement. On its own this is a major recognition of the importance of things other than trade. The WTO does not have to allow countries this right – it exists by virtue of a country being independent and self-governing. The Appellate Body also said that laws aimed at protecting sea turtles were a legitimate exception to the GATT prohibition on quotas, but only as long as the turtle-related ban was applied in a non-discriminatory way, meaning that the ban on turtle-harming shrimp shouldn't be imposed on some countries and not on others. Uneven application of the rule would violate the most favoured nation rule.

The US ended up losing the shrimp case for this reason. It had applied its turtle-safety ban on shrimp in a discriminatory fashion because it provided countries in the western hemisphere – primarily in the Caribbean – with technical and financial assist-ance in order to adhere to the turtle safety rules. The US also accorded a longer transition period for fishermen from western hemisphere countries to start using the turtle exclusion devices when harvesting shrimp. These advantages had not been extended to the four Asian countries which had brought the claim through the WTO courts. This was arbitrary and unjustified discrimin-ation, contradicting the rules of the GATT. The Appellate Body required the US to recognize foreign attempts to prevent harm to turtles that were equivalent in effectiveness to those which were contemplated under the US law. In other words, the US was compelled to adopt a shrimp ban that was more flexible in its application, in particular one that would accommodate legit-imate efforts to protect turtles such as those undertaken by the Asian complainants.

While the case was lost on what was essentially a legal tech-nicality, the WTO had made an important point in deciding that the turtle-safety ban, an attempt to conserve exhaustible natu-ral resources, would have justified the violation of GATT by the US. The Appellate Body clarified that WTO members can adopt laws to protect endangered species. It even went as far as saying that members should do this, particularly when it is required by other international treaties relating to the environment. Establish-ing that countries can adopt these types of laws without violating WTO rules was one thing, but urging that countries should adopt them was something else. The WTO, through the Appellate Body, was making a clear pro-environmental declaration, something for which the WTO is not well known. As long as these laws are imposed in an even-handed manner, environmental protection trumps free trade. Despite the fact that the US lost, the shrimp–turtle dispute has rightly been viewed as a victory for the environmental movement. The US went on to apply the ban more evenly, to the delight of sea turtles and environmentalists the world over. It is also interesting to note that, in rendering this decision, the Appellate Body allowed the US to impose an import restriction on the basis of a good's production process, rather than on the nature of the product itself. This is the so-called 'product versus process' distinction which we will come back to shortly.

Another species of marine life had been the focus of an earlier dispute brought under the GATT before the WTO itself came into existence as an organization. Heard in 1991, the tuna–dolphin case continues to captivate the public because of its treatment of the interplay between environmental protection and free trade. Like turtles, dolphins are at risk from nets used to harvest tuna in the tropical waters of the Pacific Ocean. Dolphins are also an endangered species, as well as a species of mammal that is known to possess intelligence. The US enacted a law that prohibited imports of tuna that were caught in a manner that did not meet US standards for the protection of dolphins. As a consequence of the ban, Mexico brought a complaint under the previous GATT system because its tuna ships did not meet the requirements.

The panel in the tuna–dolphin dispute, which was heard under the old, less formal dispute-settlement rules, ultimately decided that the US could not ban imports of tuna from Mexico simply because Mexican laws on the way tuna was produced did not satisfy US requirements. The US could have imposed its rules on the quality of the tuna, but not on the way it was 'produced', meaning the way it was caught, capturing the tension of the 'product versus process' distinction mentioned above. Furthermore, it was decided that GATT did not allow one country to enact trade laws for the purpose of enforcing its own domestic laws on another country, even where this was done to protect animal health or exhaustible natural resources like dolphins. If a country was allowed to do this, the panel reasoned, any country could ban imports of a product from another country merely because the exporting country had different environmental or health policies of its own.

Although the US lost the tuna–dolphin case, and the decision is often decried as an example of anti-environmental animus within international trade law, it is important to recognize that the panel was not asked to assess whether the US's environmental policy was sensible or not. Thus the panel was careful not to establish itself as an international authority on environmental law. Showing some sensitivity to endangered creatures, the panel did say that the US was allowed to specify that tuna caught according to its dolphin standards should be labelled 'dolphin safe', leaving it to consumers to choose whether or not to buy it. This did not violate the GATT because it was designed to prevent deceptive advertising practices on all tuna, whether domestic or imported. Some of the rationale of this decision found its way into later WTO agreements on technical standards. These agreements curtail member countries' freedom to restrict trade unduly by imposing excessive product safety or testing standards.

More recently, China attempted to use environmental protection as a justification for its export ban on rare earths like tungsten and molybdenum. It argued that its export restrictions on these valuable substances – important for their use in making components of electronic gadgets like mobile phones – were essential because of environmental pollution associated with the mining of the metals. The pollution from mining had to be prevented, so the Chinese said, because it was harmful to human health, another one of the GATT's General Exceptions to the imposition of quantitative restrictions. China also claimed that it had to limit exports of the rare earths because of the need to conserve an exhaustible natural resource, namely the metals themselves. The WTO panel ruled against China, siding with the US and EU, which had complained because of the inaccessibility of the rare metals on world markets due to China's hoarding. The export ban was not viewed as necessary to fulfil these environmental objectives, in large part because China appeared to be quite content to continue extracting the metals from the ground on an industrial scale for use (or storage) domestically, which made its environmental claims look empty. If the Chinese were truly worried about the environmental impact of tungsten and molybdenum mining, then why didn't they cut back on it and leave the stuff in the ground?

Given the worldwide alarm over climate change – and the notorious difficulties in establishing precisely what causes this phenomenon, including a wide range of economic activity – it is likely that environmental policies will be used as justifications for a greater number of trade-related laws in the future. It will be interesting to see how the WTO, as a trade authority lacking any express competence in environmental or even scientific matters, will deal with these pressing and divisive issues.

The incredibly broad categories of public morals and public order have also been used as a defence to trade barriers under the WTO's services agreement, the General Agreement on Trade in Services (GATS), created in 1995 along with the WTO to liberalize trade in services (which were not covered under the GATT). The dispute between Antigua and the US over online gambling, which we looked at in chapter 3 because of its inventive punishment, involved an attempted justification on the basis of upholding public morality. Antigua challenged US laws which prohibited the remote supply of gambling and betting services, including those offered on the Internet. While this violated commitments that the US had undertaken under the GATS, the US claimed that these domestic laws were nevertheless justified because they were necessary to protect public morals and to maintain public order, words found in the text of the GATS. But what do these concepts mean? Public morals and public order are such vague terms that they can mean almost whatever the country relying on them wants them to. The panel itself acknowledged this, stating that the notion of public morals and public order can vary in time and space and depend on a range of factors, including prevailing social, cultural, ethical and religious values. This flexibility is one way that the WTO manages to stay relatively up to date.

In attempting to make some sense of these highly indeterminate justifications for breaking WTO rules, the panel resorted to an ordinary dictionary, concluding that the two concepts (morality and order) overlapped to a degree and, taken together, they were generally intended to capture genuine threats to the fundamental interests of society. Was online gambling such a threat? The US said that Internet gambling could lead to organized crime and money laundering, as well as fraud. It also represented a serious risk to children as well as human health because of the greater risk it posed of addiction, which can destabilize families and is very difficult to control, unlike gambling in actual casinos. These concerns were accepted as legitimate by the panel and this was upheld by the Appellate Body, which also ruled that the US ban was necessary to address these harms. Establishing necessity is not easy; it basically means that there was no other way possible to achieve the goal. The US ended up losing this case

SEAL PRODUCTS

In one of the most controversial recent WTO decisions invoking the General Exceptions of the GATT, the WTO courts were required to consider the legitimacy of a country's laws grounded in ethical beliefs about cruelty towards animals. In 2009, Canada brought a complaint against the EU through the WTO dispute settlement system, because of a ban imposed by Europe on the importation and sale of all seal-related products. Europe maintained an exception for seals caught by Indigenous communities in the Arctic such as the Inuit, but it applied the exception only to seal products originating from Greenland, not Canada. Canada contested the uneven application of the exception as discriminatory. Iceland and Norway later joined the proceedings, asserting along with Canada that the ban violated the GATT. Europe attempted to argue that the ban on seal products was justified on the basis of the GATT's exception for measures necessary for the protection of animal life or health, as well as public morals. Predominately using firearms, as opposed to traditional methods like clubbing, Indigenous groups in Canada hunt roughly 90,000 seals per year to sell commercially. Rendering its decision in late 2013, the WTO panel stated that Europe's ban on seal products was justified on the basis of public morals, specifically the outrage in Europe over the way seals were killed and consumed by the Indigenous peoples. Europe was able to defend the ban on the basis that there was no less trade-restrictive way to deal with the public's response to what was viewed as inhumane behaviour. However, it could not explain the uneven application of the exception – there was no justification for allowing seal products caught by Indigenous groups in Greenland but not the ones caught by those in Canada. The latter, Europe claimed, were more commercial rather than subsistence in nature, but it did not provide sufficient evidence to support this distinction. While animal welfare activists celebrated the decision in that it legitimized an animal welfare exception to international trade, seal-hunting communities in Canada have been enraged at what they see as hypocrisy on the part of the EU. They claim that the ban on seal products produced in a culturally traditional way is a double standard, given the commercial scale of meat eating by Europeans. They see the WTO's allowance of the public morals defence as discrimination against one particular way of killing animals that happens not to fit within European cultural practices. If killing seals for their meat on ice floes in the Arctic is immoral, couldn't the same argument be made concerning the slaughtering of chickens or pigs on industrialized farms in France and Germany? As soon as morality is asserted as the basis for anything it becomes almost impossible to establish any kind of standard by which equivalent rules of conduct can be set. Morality, like religion, is a highly subjective concept that is heavily rooted in culture and tradition.

anyway, much as in the shrimp case, because it applied the ban on online gambling unevenly. While the US prohibited online card games from Antigua, it was quite content to allow online betting on domestic horse racing, suggesting a hidden protectionist aim.

China attempted to rely on a public moral defence found in both GATT and GATS to support its restrictions on imported films, DVDs and various publications including magazines and books. The US initiated a complaint against China through the WTO courts in 2009 arguing that China's laws were unfairly discriminating against US movies and publications because they essentially required that importation and distribution of these products must be done in conjunction with a registered Chinese entity, the idea being that only such an organization would be able to identify whether or not foreign entertainment could undermine Chinese cultural identity, something that it felt was more important than its free trade commitments under the WTO. The Appellate Body ultimately ruled that the public morals defence could have been used in this way, but that China had failed to demonstrate that the import and distribution controls were necessary for fulfilling the goal of upholding public morals. First, a less trade-restrictive way of protecting Chinese culture may plausibly have been available, for example, simply by having a Chinese official reviewing foreign publications for appropriate content. But, more importantly, the WTO court clarified that the protection of public morals and public order requires some explanation – it cannot simply be asserted. If China had believed strongly that foreign films, music and magazines represented a threat to its cultural identity, then this would have had to be shown convincingly. One of the problems with a defence as fuzzy as upholding public order or public morals (which may well be viewed as synonyms for culture) is that the type of evidence needed to ground such a claim would be incredibly difficult to substantiate, unlike scientific evidence justifying a health or environmental exception. What is culture, anyway, and is it for the WTO to decide? To its credit, the WTO court seemed to avoid answering this question directly.

When evaluating a public policy-based exception for a violation of WTO law, it is not enough to identify a particular non-trade concern that matters to the country enacting the offending law. The country must show that the law was not applied in a discriminatory or uneven fashion, meaning that it was applied in the same way to imports from all countries. For public morals and animal health, the country applying the disputed measure also has to demonstrate that there was not a less trade-restrictive method that could have fulfilled the same objective – this is what is meant by the word 'necessary'. This will involve a weighing and balancing of various different regulatory actions that the government could have taken and the effects that these may or may not have had on international trade in affected products. The concept of 'necessary' found in three of the specified GATT exceptions (public morals, health and compliance with various regulations) is complicated and has a long history in WTO disputes. More strict than the 'relating to' standard, 'necessary' contemplates the lack of a reasonably available alternative that is either WTO-consistent or, if not consistent, less trade-restrictive than the one which was actually adopted. If the complaining party is able to present such an alternative method for achieving the designated policy goal, then the measure at issue will fail the analysis under the GATT General Exceptions. The flexibility and discretion inherent in the application of the necessity test may be viewed as a useful counterpoint to the relatively narrow grounds covered by the General Exceptions themselves.

So, in the shrimp–turtle dispute, the US could have achieved the same objective – protecting sea turtles – through a less rigidly applied law regarding the turtle exclusion devices. Instead of an outright ban, the US government could have adopted a more consultative, flexible approach wherein they evaluated the particular shrimp-harvesting practices of each country in its individual context. Because they did not, this amounted to a disguised restriction on international trade.

It is crucial that, when using an exception that is specified in the GATT (or the GATS), the member country must do so in a manner that is honest and forthright. The exceptions should not be abused. This is often described as a principle of 'good faith', a term which lawyers love because it covers all sorts of under-handed behaviour. So, a compromise must be struck between the right of a member to invoke an exception and the rights guaranteed in the rest of the WTO law – like tariff bindings and non-discrimination. The WTO panels and Appellate Body are tasked with maintaining this delicate balance, which in many ways encapsulates the essential conflict that exists at the heart of the relationship between the WTO as an organization and the sovereign rights of its members. In performing this role the WTO courts are able to guard against the exploitation of alleged policy goals as tools of protectionism. In an era of growing awareness of issues like climate change, health and the importance of cultural identity, this is likely to become an increasingly difficult and vital exercise.

Economic emergency exceptions

Sometimes free trade is simply too difficult for some countries to bear. This may not be the consequence of particular environ-mental or other social issues of importance to a member state, but merely that the country's economy or a particular sector within it is not strong enough to withstand foreign competition. While an approach focused on strict economic efficiency would tell us that such industries should be allowed to die to make way for more robust ones that better serve the interest of consumers in offering lower-cost or higher-quality goods, the reality is that sometimes this process can have devastating effects. Mass unemployment and social degradation is undesirable, even if it means that someone somewhere else in the world is better off. In situations where strict adherence to the WTO rules on trade liberalization can be too harmful to a member state, the rules may be broken, subject to a few key requirements.

The procedure of rule-breaking when the harm is too great is called safeguards. It is one of the most important policy tools for countries to maintain their conformity with the overall regime of the WTO. It is often described as a 'safety valve' because it allows members to get out of their international trade obligations when things get too tough and serious harm can result. This is particularly important for politicians who would otherwise have to justify to their constituents why factories are closing and people are out of work because of some obscure international treaty that benefits suppliers on the other side of the world.

Under the safeguard regime, a WTO member may restrict imports of products temporarily if its domestic industry is injured or threatened with injury that has been caused by a 'surge' in imports. Unlike the injury that we discussed in relation to subsidies and dumping in the previous chapter, the injury needed to justify these safeguard restrictions must be serious. An import surge may be a real or absolute increase in imports of a particular product, or it can be relative – meaning an increase in the imports' share of a shrinking market, even if the import quantity has not increased. This alone can be damaging.

Industries or companies can ask their governments to initiate safeguard actions in response to these situations. But, in order for this to be done, WTO members must adhere to the rules set out by the WTO. As with countervailing measures for subsidies and anti-dumping duties for dumping, safeguard actions require investigations by national authorities. These procedures must be transparent and non-arbitrary. The investigating authorities in the country intending to impose the safeguards must announce publicly when hearings are going to take place and provide opportunity for interested parties, like the exporters from other countries as well as companies in the importing country, to present evidence about how harmful their imports are or are not. This should include evidence relating to whether the safeguard measure is in the public interest as a restriction on free trade.

WTO safeguard rules establish criteria for determining whether a 'serious injury' is being caused or is threatened to be caused, including the factors which must be considered in assessing the impact of imports on the domestic industry in question. Unsurprisingly, the standard of serious injury is very high. This could be demonstrated by increases in unemployment, declining profitability, share value or bankruptcies. There is also a causation requirement – it is not enough that the domestic industry is suffering; the suffering must be the result of the import surge. A causal link must be established between the increase in imports and the injury sustained by the industry. Other factors that could have contributed must be discounted, such as changing consumer tastes, high prices or excessive wages, meaning essentially poor business practices. This would equate safeguards with classic protectionism, which is forbidden in the WTO universe.

Once allowed, a safeguard measure must only be applied to the extent necessary to prevent or remedy the serious injury and to allow the industry to adjust to the increase in imports. The safeguards should not reduce the quantity of imports below the annual average for the last three years for which import statistics are available, unless a higher reduction can be clearly justified on the grounds of the potential severity of the injury. In order for safeguards to be lawful, the increase in imports must be recent, sudden and sharp. If these criteria are not satisfied, then there will be no economic emergency, which is the foundation of the safeguard regime. This also requires that the import surge must be unforeseen, the idea being that if operators in the domestic industry had known about it in advance, they would have been able to deal with the issue by restructuring their commercial activities.

ARGENTINA FOOTWEAR

In 1998, Argentina became concerned about the influx of shoes from Europe, so it decided to impose safeguard measures in the form of increased duties, beyond the levels it had committed to under its GATT bound tariffs. Argentina wanted to impose legitimate emergency measures because it had liberalized many sectors of its economy to international trade under the regional MERCOSUR (the Southern Common Market) agreement with other South American countries too rapidly, leading to economic crisis. But MERCOSUR had no safeguard regime, so Argentina attempted to justify its imposition of emergency tariffs under the WTO instead. The EU complained, arguing that under WTO law Argentina's safeguards had to be imposed evenly against injury-causing imports from all countries, including other South American ones within MERCOSUR. The Appellate Body agreed with this assessment, ruling that Argentina's safeguard regime on European shoes was illegal because it discriminated against European shoes without justification – the European imports of shoes were no more damaging than those from other South American countries. The Argentina footwear case illustrates that the WTO is in many ways ahead of some of the regional trade agreements because of its sophistication in having a comprehensive safety valve mechanism for emergency situations like this one. It also demonstrates that the removal of trade barriers for certain goods sometimes requires more well-thought-out transition periods so that countries can adapt to the changes at their own pace. If Argentina had lowered its tariffs on shoe imports more gradually, there may not have been such an acute need for emergency measures through safeguards. This situation thus captures the essential purpose of the WTO's emergency measures regime – in many respects it is intended to address circumstances where countries bite off more than they can chew in terms of their international trade obligations, or to use a more apt metaphor, when they try on shoes that are a few sizes too big.

When a WTO member country restricts the imports from another WTO country in order to safeguard the producers in one of its domestic industries, it should give something back in return. This is because safeguards are meant to counter fair trade, not unfair trade as in the case of subsidies or dumping.

The importing country should enter into consultation with the exporting country to come up with some kind of compensation. If no agreement is reached, then the exporting country can retaliate by taking an equivalent action, such as raising the tariffs on exports from the country that is imposing the safeguard measure. The retaliating country often has to wait several years before it is allowed to do this with the WTO's blessing. This whole process is overseen by a special committee within the WTO.

By the end of 2013, more than 240 safeguard measure investigations had been reported to the WTO, with about half of these resulting in the actual imposition of safeguards. India has been the most frequent user of safeguards, demonstrating its difficulty in adapting to globalization. If safeguards are imposed in violation of the special procedures, complaints can be brought through the WTO's dispute settlement system. Given the danger that China posed with respect to import surges in WTO countries because of its vast manufacturing capacity, a special safeguard procedure was established for Chinese exports as part of China's terms of accession to the WTO. This special safeguard mechanism, which expired in 2013, established a lower threshold for the application of safeguards, including a lower standard of injury, against Chinese imports than against those from all other countries.

In addition to the safeguards measures, the WTO also allows members to transgress their obligations for 'balance of payment' purposes. Essentially balance of payments incorporates all of a country's expenditures and income between itself and the rest of the world. If expenditures are higher than income for a prolonged period this can be very damaging to a country's economy. In order to deal with such problems, countries are allowed to limit the outflow of money from within their territory so that they do not become too indebted to other countries or financial institutions. One of the ways they can do this is by restricting imports, which would normally be a violation of the GATT's prohibition on quantitative restrictions. The balance of payments exception therefore enables a country to restrict its inward trade flows when it is carrying too much debt to the point that it has a serious insufficiency of monetary reserves. Under the guidance of the IMF, balance of payments problems can be resolved by non-trade methods, notably through short-term loans. Given the competency of the IMF in this sphere, the WTO now tends to take a hands-off approach to balance of payments matters or, when it does get involved, it consults directly with the IMF. The WTO did this when India imposed quantitative restrictions on various products in 1999 because of its serious balance of payments deficit.

The WTO's relationship with the IMF is a complex one, with the WTO focusing on trade and the IMF on money and currency exchange, as well as sovereign debt relief in the form of temporary loans. The overlapping competencies of the two organizations are seen most obviously in relation to currency wars discussed earlier, which have dominated international political and economic debates in recent years. The WTO has preferred not to touch this hot-button issue, saying that it is up to the IMF to police currency manipulation. So the GATT states simply that WTO members that are also members of the IMF should observe their IMF obligations, meaning they should not artificially weaken their currencies to make their goods cheaper. A formal currency manipulation complaint has yet to be brought through the WTO and may not be for some time, as the world recovers from the recent global financial crisis.

National security

Perhaps the most important policy justification for departing from WTO obligations is that relating to national security.

National security-based exceptions are found in the GATT and the GATS, and despite their obvious significance in terms of structuring domestic laws, these exceptions have not yet been the subject of a WTO dispute.

National security can have a direct impact on international trade in several instances. Countries may consider it necessary to restrict trade in order to protect strategic domestic production capabilities from competition with imports. Deciding which industries are deserving of this type of protection is up to each country, and the determination often has a significant political dimension. It will typically include industries equipping the military, energy and staple foods. Countries may also seek to use trade-based sanctions as an instrument of foreign policy against other states. In the modern era this is often done at the behest of the UN and its Security Council, which authorizes military or other intervention in response to international security crises. In such situations, the international community can agree to cease exports to particular countries that have been deemed to be acting against the interests of peace. Embargoes were imposed in this way recently against Iran, which had been developing nuclear weapons technology that posed a risk to the security of a number of countries in the Middle East; and Russia, when it annexed part of Ukraine. Relatedly, countries may seek to prohibit the export of weapons or other products of military use to countries they may consider to be enemies.

Accordingly, nothing in the GATT prevents a WTO member from taking any action which it (meaning the member country) considers necessary for the protection of its essential security interests. One of the interesting features of this provision is the phrase 'that it considers necessary', which effectively means that it is entirely up to the discretion of each member country to take action for national security purposes. The country does not have to ask the WTO for permission, and the WTO cannot inquire into what those security interests are or how they have been established, meaning what intelligence has been used. This part of GATT is often described as the 'all bets off' rule. If national security is at risk, then trade obligations, however sincere or economically important, simply don't stack up. If you think about it, this rule is really self-evident. It would be difficult to imagine any country opening up its high-level security concerns to the scrutiny of an international body. It's not very likely you would ever see a team of bureaucrats in Geneva giving orders to the Pentagon or MI6. This is why it's virtually impossible to imagine that the WTO would get involved if Russia attempts to make good on its threat to use the WTO dispute settlement system to counter US sanctions imposed on it for the Crimean conflict.

The problem with allowing a country this much leeway to abandon its WTO obligations is that it could be exploited as a justification for protectionism, although we would hope that this doesn't happen too often. Still, this is problematic precisely because a number of countries maintain embargoes for political reasons, such as the well-known US policy of isolationism towards Cuba, which is showing signs of abating at the time of writing. The US's stance towards Cuba led to a disagreement between the US and the European Union in 1996. The US Helms–Burton Act allowed US nationals to bring legal action in US courts against foreign companies that dealt in US property that had been confiscated by the Cuban government. Some of these companies were in Europe, and the EU contended that this law was inconsistent with the US's obligations under the WTO, wherein the WTO dispute settlement system is supposed to be the final arbiter of any trade-related dispute between WTO members. The US countered that this issue was a diplomatic and security matter, not a trade one, and was therefore fundamentally outside the WTO regime. The EU eventually backed off.

While this type of situation can lead to diplomatic squabbles among WTO members regarding exactly when something becomes an essential security matter and therefore justifies under-mining free trade, it is a vital feature of the WTO's acknowl-edgement of national sovereignty underneath the framework of multilateral trade commitments. If the national security excep-tion did not exist, it is likely that there would be no WTO at all.

The public interest exceptions we have looked at in this chapter apply to regulations on all sorts of traded goods, but they are just as likely to affect rules on trade in services – things like banking and telecommunications. International commercial activities in these services can pose a threat to national security just as they can threaten public morals and culture. These services are also vital sources of economic growth. The WTO's treatment of this important and growing sphere of international trade will be examined in the next chapter.

6

Not just things: the liberalization of trade in services

One of the great achievements of the WTO was the expansion of its coverage to encompass things other than goods, meaning physical objects that can be loaded onto ships, whether they are manufactured like cars, or commodities like coffee or bananas. Economic activity relating to non-physical goods is captured by the general category of services, which includes things like banking, transportation and tourism. Services are the fastest-growing sector of the global economy, accounting for more than two thirds of worldwide economic output as reflected in GDP. Services make up an even greater portion of economic activity in wealthy countries, sometimes as much as seventy percent or more in advanced countries like the UK, which continues to experience a decline in manufacturing, for now at least. With the comparative advantage of manufactured goods shifting to low-wage countries in the developing world, developed countries became eager to improve their advantage in the services which tend to attract higher-skilled and higher-paid workers. Services also account for more than one third of global employment, with up to three quarters of employment in rich countries.

Yet services still amount to only twenty percent of international trade. This relatively poor showing is despite the Internet and mobile phone revolution of the past twenty years which has made communications to all corners of the world unimaginably cheap and efficient. So you would think that trade in services would be as common as trade in goods.

The relatively small portion of international trade made up of services reveals that there are still many legal impediments to their free flow around the world. This was one of the primary motivations for the negotiation of a services agreement, the General Agreement on Trade in Services (GATS), to complement the GATT during the run-up to the creation of the WTO in the mid-1990s. Another factor in the inception of the GATS was the privatization and deregulation movements that swept many countries in the West during the 1970s and 1980s. While a number of key service industries were highly regulated during the post-war period, the popularity of small government politics associated primarily with Ronald Reagan in the US and Margaret Thatcher in the UK led to regulatory reform and the elimination of state monopolies in industries like telecommunications and transportation. This exposed many more services industries to domestic competition. International competition was the next logical step.

The General Agreement on Trade in Services (GATS)

Setting rules for something is difficult when you're not quite sure what that thing is. When you make a call on your mobile phone, are you using a good? What about when you turn on your TV to watch a programme? A phone is a manufactured product, as is a TV. They are both physical objects that may well have been assembled in another country to be shipped to your country and ultimately to the store where you purchased them. But what about the phone or television signal, meaning the broadcast of data as electromagnetic waves? Are these also goods? And how about the electricity used to power your TV, or to charge the battery of your mobile phone? While it would take a physicist (or possibly even a philosopher, depending on how far you take it) to tell us exactly what photons or electrons are made of, it would be difficult to argue in a serious way that these are physical things, even though they have measurable mass. They are certainly not objects like vodka or bananas.

Although relying on physical goods for their delivery to consumers, telecommunications like mobile phone and television signals are properly described as services, and accordingly fall outside the GATT's coverage. Instead they are regulated by the GATS. The GATS is the only global system of rules governing international trade in services. Although it is now more than twenty years old, the GATS is still a young treaty, at least compared to the GATT, which dates from the 1940s. When the idea of bringing rules on services into the multilateral framework of the WTO was discussed in the 1980s, many countries were opposed because it was believed that an international treaty in this area could profoundly threaten a country's capacity to regulate itself. Rules on services, it was felt, penetrate far deeper into economic policymaking than rules on goods, because services tend to be more heavily regulated than goods. Think about the way in which lawyers, doctors or accountants are subject to training, quality control and licensing in a way that things like tyres or windows are not.

In order to assuage these concerns from the WTO members, the GATS was designed with a very high degree of flexibility, unlike the GATT. This is now thought to be the GATS' greatest strength as well as a crucial weakness as an instrument of liberalizing international trade. The GATS' flexibility comes from a highly circumscribed scope of coverage and an individualized rather than general approach to rules.

It is often said that if you ask two economists a question you will get three different answers. Well, if you ask a hundred or

more trade lawyers (one for each member country) for a definition you will get more than a thousand answers. Since it was so
difficult to define trade in something as insubstantial and varied
as services, the GATS negotiators decided not to. Instead they
came up with four 'modes of supply' of services, which they felt
would encompass all of the types of economic activity that are
captured in the understanding of services. Separating services
into four categories would also facilitate segmented (effectively
incomplete) legal commitments for countries that were nervous
about exposing too many of their industries to foreign competition. Commitments to liberalize service markets could be made
under one mode and not another, depending on the particular
economic needs and concerns of each member.

The first mode of supply of services is cross-border supply.
This is where a service from within the territory of one WTO
member is used by someone in the territory of another member.
So if you phone an accountant in the US from your house in
London to get an opinion about any income tax you might owe
to the US government, you are engaging in this mode of supply
of service – as the consumer of course, not the supplier. The
accountant is supplying the services to a consumer (you) across
international borders. This type of service delivery is subjected to
very few controls by member countries partly because it is very
difficult to regulate services tendered remotely over the Internet
and phone.

The second mode of supply is consumption abroad. This is
where a person travels from the territory of one member into
the territory of another member for the purpose of using or
consuming a service in that foreign country. So, when you want
to get plastic surgery in California but you live in Dublin, you
fly to California to consume this medical service abroad, return-
ing home when you have had the procedure. There are very few
limitations on this mode of service supply because it poses little

to no risk to the domestic economy; in fact, foreign short-term consumers of privately supplied services are quite welcome in most countries.

The third mode of supply of services is that in which a company with a head office or main place of business in the territory of one WTO member establishes an office or branch/ subsidiary in the territory of another member. So, if you live in Sydney and open an account at a local branch of a Hong Kong bank, you are consuming a service that has been supplied via the commercial presence mode of delivery. The commercial presence mode of services delivery has been subjected to numerous restrictions by WTO members because of the concern that the presence of foreign companies in certain sensitive sectors, like telecommunications and finance, can undermine national security, as well as potentially lead to an unhealthy reliance on foreign capital that can easily be removed at the whim of shareholders in other countries.

Finally, the fourth mode captures the movement of natural persons, meaning humans not corporations. This category contemplates situations where people travel to and stay temporarily in another country for the purpose of providing a service in that foreign country, not to consume one as in the plastic surgery example. So, if a British engineer travels to Dubai in the United Arab Emirates to work on an office tower project for a few weeks or months, this person will be engaging in the fourth mode of supply. The movement of natural persons is perhaps the most controversial of the four modes and the one where members have been most reluctant to make commitments. This is because allowing aliens to enter and work in your country can be politically unpopular. There is a perception that foreigners take the jobs of local workers, rather than contributing to the economy, something that may be true in some countries but more often than not is exaggerated for political reasons. In many countries foreign workers are an essential source of skilled labour. India has been particularly strident in encouraging other WTO members to liberalize their services sectors to the movement of natural persons because of its large, highly skilled, English-speaking labour force. In order to limit the scope of this mode of supply under GATS, the agreement makes it clear that commitments in this area do not apply to any laws affecting people who seek permanent access to the employment market of a member, nor does it apply to citizenship or residency. GATS Mode 4 only deals with short-term stays of foreign employees. Indeed, as mentioned in chapter 1, the WTO has done almost nothing in terms of international labour mobility.

FOREIGN DIRECT INVESTMENT IN SERVICES

The WTO has no specific role in regulating or liberalizing foreign direct investment (FDI). FDI involves the activity of multinational corporations, meaning companies that have affiliates in countries outside their home state of incorporation, and is a major component of the global economy as well as an essential feature of globalization. There was almost US $1.5 trillion in global FDI outflows (money leaving one country to be invested in another one) in 2013. This is not trade because the products created by the company do not move across borders; instead, the company itself moves. As you might imagine, having a company enter your country, along with its managers, employees and distinct ways of doing business, is quite a bit more intrusive than simply allowing the products which it produces to pass through your borders as exports. This is one of the reasons that FDI tends to be more heavily regulated than trade, with services even more so because of the already tightly regulated nature of many high-skilled services professions like lawyers and doctors. Furthermore, unlike trade, FDI tends to be regulated bilaterally rather than multilaterally – it is subject to laws found in agreements between two countries known as bilateral investment treaties, or BITs. There are now many thousands of these instruments, which grant protection to foreign investors that are worried about host countries interfering with their assets, either by overburdening them with

discriminatory laws, or by taking them outright in expropria-
tion without compensation. While BITs may help investors that
have already set up shop in a foreign country, they don't actually
grant foreign investors the right to establish themselves overseas.
BITs are about protection of investments, not the liberalization
of global investment flows. In that sense, FDI is nowhere near
as free as trade, where WTO members are entitled to sell goods
to other WTO members, subject to agreed tariffs. Still, FDI is
captured by the GATS Mode 3 of services delivery: the commercial presence supply of services. So, through this limited provision
in the GATS, the WTO does have a degree of regulatory control
over FDI, at least in relation to services. Of course, the extent to
which the GATS has contributed to the liberalization of FDI in
services has depended upon the number of commercial presence
commitments made by WTO members. While progress has been
made in eliminating ownership and other restrictions in fields
such as financial services and telecommunications, many countries still impose numerous barriers, often linked to the amount
of money that foreign companies must bring with them into host
states when they open a branch. It is their right as WTO members
to dictate the nature of the restrictions they wish to place on
companies entering their borders. So it is best to see GATS as a
good foundation for services FDI, with much more progress need-
ing to be made.

One additional limit on the coverage of the GATS involves
governmental services. Obligations contained in the GATS do
not apply to services supplied 'in the exercise of governmental
authority'. These are defined as any services which are supplied
neither on a commercial basis (meaning to make money) nor in
competition with one or more service suppliers (meaning that
there is a monopoly). Obviously the type of services that will
fit into this category is going to depend on both the economic
structure and political heritage of each WTO member. Things
like police and firemen would likely be viewed as governmental-
type services in most countries. But, increasingly, services that
traditionally might have been viewed as governmental, like health
care, education, postal services and garbage collection, have

widely become privatized and are now within the economic activity of profit-seeking companies. Services paid for by the government in the performance of its governmental authority but supplied by a private party, such as the outsourcing of security services to supplement police activities, would also fall outside the sphere of the GATS. Such arrangements would be covered instead by the WTO's Agreement on Government Procurement, which is optional for WTO members and currently has fewer than thirty signatory countries.

The extent to which services previously supplied in the exercise of governmental authority have now become fields of commercial activity is itself a subject of fierce debate. The recent sell-off of the postal services in the UK and Canada has drawn bitter criticism, especially from organized labour groups who fear that commercial control will result in downsizing and job losses. In the US, the idea has been mooted of turning public institutions like jails into businesses operated by companies, and this has also been dramatized in awful science fiction movies like *Death Race* (2008). The WTO has no control over these decisions by sovereign countries. However, should a government seek to outsource or privatize such services internationally, then it will be bound by its GATS commitments. Whereas governments had once been in the business of running services like rail networks and airlines, privatization has become an established feature of many market-oriented countries in the West. In countries with a tradition of centralized command economies and state-owned enterprises, the concept of governmental service will naturally be much wider, encompassing a much broader range of activities. In this sense, the carve-out of services supplied in the exercise of governmental authority reflects the market-oriented bias of the GATS, and indeed of the WTO itself, which was created essentially by Americans and Europeans.

Selective commitments

Unlike the GATT, which applies across the board to all members and all goods, the GATS agreement is something of an empty shell without the specific, optional commitments made by the member countries. GATS contains a most favoured nation commitment (the promise to treat things from all foreign countries the same) as well as provisions on transparency, but its national treatment guarantee (the promise to treat foreign things the same as local ones) is extended only to the degree that each country wishes. Members list the service industries in which they are willing to promise non-discrimination against foreign suppliers, and even within each industry members are free to dictate the particular mode of delivery they wish to include. This information is contained in each member's services schedule, which is similar to the tariff bindings schedule that goes with the GATT.

So, for example, Canada's schedule of services commitments under GATS might include legal services commitments under cross-border supply, consumption abroad and movement of natural persons, but not commercial presence. This would mean that Canada is willing to allow foreign lawyers to give advice to Canadians over the phone or Internet, to have foreigners enter Canada to receive legal advice while there, to have foreign lawyers enter Canada to work there temporarily, but not to have a foreign law firm establish an office there. In reality, Canada allows all four of these modes of delivery for legal services, although it has all kinds of educational requirements and cumbersome certification procedures that still make it quite difficult to practise law in Canada compared to most other developed countries. It should be noted that GATS also encourages countries to recognize qualifications obtained by professionals, such as lawyers and accountants, in other countries.

Sometimes countries may disagree as to whether they have or have not made a national treatment commitment in their GATS schedule. In the dispute relating to China's commitments on the distribution of magazines and audiovisual products, which I mentioned in the previous chapter, China had argued that 'sound recording distribution services' did not extend to sound recordings that were distributed by electronic means, but only distribution in physical form, as in CDs. The WTO courts ended up ruling against China, determining that a reasonable understanding of the phrase 'sound recording distribution services' does in fact contemplate electronic as well as physical forms of delivery. In making this determination, the Appellate Body relied on the way this phrase had been used by other WTO members in making their services commitments, and the fact that the words were sufficiently generic that what they applied to may change over time. In short, 'distribution' could evolve to mean something different in line with the rise of the Internet and the popularity of music downloading.

The selective coverage of the national treatment non-discrimination guarantee is the embodiment of the GATS' flexibility and the cornerstone of the WTO's principle of 'progressive liberalization'. While member countries of the WTO do not have to promise to open up their markets to trade in services, they do undertake at least to consider doing so in the future. Countries can also backtrack on commitments they have made, provided that they give enough notice and offer compensation in the form of increased access to other services if there has been harm suffered as a consequence of the revocation. Negotiations for greater liberalization, meaning allowing more and more industries to be open to foreign service providers, began in 2000 and continue to this day in the Doha Round. The objective is to widen the scope of coverage as much as possible, much as tariffs were reduced over the years.

As under GATT, both the most favoured nation and national treatment obligations of the GATS also require a 'likeness' test. In order to ascertain whether or not there has been discrimination, either between two other WTO members or between the member itself and all other members, it must be determined whether the services or services suppliers concerned are 'like services' or 'like services suppliers'. Herein lies another crucial difference between the WTO's treatment of goods under GATT and services under GATS. The non-discrimination guarantees in GATS apply both to the service as well as the person or entity supplying it, whereas under GATT the guarantee only applies to the product itself. For example, a Brazilian law dictating that all legal services offered in Brazil must be offered in Portuguese would unfairly discriminate against foreign legal services. A Brazilian law dictating that all legal services in Brazil must be provided by lawyers with Brazilian law degrees would discriminate against foreign legal services suppliers.

Comparing suppliers, usually companies, is a somewhat different exercise than comparing the service itself, whether it be plumbing, painting or financial advice. While the fact that they tender the same service will be useful in establishing likeness between two providers, it is not determinative. As with the GATT, whether or not either of these comparisons is satisfied will be decided on a case-by-case basis (remember the accordion metaphor). In looking at the suppliers themselves, WTO panels and the Appellate Body have shown that this will also involve a consideration of whether or not the suppliers are in a competitive relationship with each other, although this is not necessarily sufficient to establish likeness.

In another GATS dispute involving China, this time relating to electronic payment services (meaning payments in Chinese renminbis made by debit and credit card rather than by cash or cheque), the WTO courts determined that 'likeness' under GATS had a whole range of meanings and did not require that the services be exactly the same as long as they were 'essentially or generally' the same. This reasoning is not terribly rigorous, but it is helpful in illustrating the highly discretionary nature of the likeness test for both services and services suppliers under GATS, much as we saw in chapter 2 in relation to the GATT. Indeed, disputes brought in relation to goods under GATT can and have been used by the WTO panels and Appellate Body in evaluating likeness under GATS.

Non-discrimination as to national origin of the services is only one half of the story when it comes to the scope of GATS. Under GATS, WTO members also have the option of making commitments relating to another type of trade barrier known as market access. Like 'services' itself, the GATS does not define market access barriers to trade in services, but it does provide a list of what barriers to market access constitute. These essentially consist of quantitative limits on the provision of services, either in the number of service providers in a particular industry, the value of the service transactions they can participate in, the number of people they can employ or the amount of foreign capital invested in the service supplier. If a market access commitment is made by a WTO member country (and again they don't have to make any) then these types of restrictions on services are prohibited. This is so regardless of whether the restriction is discriminatory (only applies to foreign service providers) or non-discriminatory (applies equally to foreign and local service providers).

Market access is really about liberalization of services generally, not discrimination between domestic and foreign services. For example, a restriction on the number of foreign banks allowed to set up branches is clearly a discriminatory market access barrier, whereas a licence issued by the government for all new banks based on the minimum amount of capitalization required would be a non-discriminatory market access barrier. So, in the US gambling dispute brought by Antigua, which we discussed in both chapters 3 and 5, the US was found to have breached its GATS market access commitment by prohibiting the supply of online gambling services. This was because the panel and later the Appellate Body found that a prohibition was just another way of maintaining a quota of zero, which was effectively a numeric limitation that constituted a market access barrier. Expanding access to markets in more services industries is intended to increase competition, either from local suppliers or from suppliers from other WTO members. Economists tell us that more competition should translate to better-quality services at lower prices, enhance employment opportunities and spur innovation. Of course, intensifying competition in services can also lead to some companies going out of business because they cannot withstand new market entrants, just as it can lead to a loss of jobs for service suppliers who are not as good or who have charged their employers or customers too much. Furthermore, some industries are believed to operate better when there is no competition. These are the so-called natural monopolies, such as rail networks. Other services, like banking and telecommunications, also raise security risks when they are operated by foreigners, so they have to be more carefully monitored by governments.

Because of these constraints on full liberalization, WTO members do not have to make market access commitments under GATS. As with national treatment, this depends on whether and to what extent a member has said that it will make a market access commitment in its schedule of commitments. This format of selective, voluntary coverage is known as a 'positive list'. This means that a country doesn't have any national treatment or market access commitments unless it takes the time and effort to list them. It has often been said that GATS would have been more effective, meaning that it would have covered more services industries and more modes of delivery in both national treatment and market access, if it had instead adopted a 'negative list' approach. This format would mean that the country automatically commits everything (national treatment and market access in all service industries and all modes) *except* for the specific types of services that it wants to omit.

Imagine that you were going grocery shopping and, instead of listing the things that you needed to buy, you started listing all of the things that you did not need to buy. Unless you took hours or even days as well as hundreds of pages of writing to do this, when you got to the store you would start grabbing everything, only pausing to be sure that you didn't pick up the few things you listed. Your cart would be full very quickly; in fact, you would most likely need many carts to get everything, depending on the size of the store.

Since GATS used a positive list style, the result has been that far fewer commitments have been made than were initially hoped for. Of course, if a negative list style had been used, it may be that GATS would never have come to exist in the first place, because WTO members would have been too worried about making sure that they excluded all of the sensitive or vulnerable sectors.

It must be understood that the GATS is not about deregulation of services. In fact, opening up the markets of some services sectors, like transportation, will actually require increased regulation so that quality and safety can be assured. GATS also expressly preserves the right of members to regulate services within their territory in order to meet national policy objectives. This can include economic interests, such as the nurturing of infant industries or preventing recession. Countries are also free to impose regulations on services for the purposes of public health and safety. These types of regulations will be explored more closely in the next chapter. GATS does require members to be open and transparent in the way that they regulate their own services industries. Each country is required to maintain its own system of administrative and judicial procedures relating to services, meaning that they must have clear and fair rules regarding licensing, qualifications, registration and other practical matters relating to the provision of services.

MEXICAN TELECOMMUNICATIONS

Most people have heard of Carlos Slim, the Mexican billionaire investor and philanthropist. Among his many business forays, one of Slim's most lucrative investments was the telecommunications company Telmex, which he bought from the Mexican government in 1990 as part of the Mexican government's privatization initiative. The shift away from state control of the sector didn't prevent the US from bringing a complaint through the WTO courts alleging that Mexico still maintained anti-competitive market access barriers in its telecommunications industry, making it difficult for new entrants in a manner that violated the country's commitments under GATS. In particular, the US argued that Mexico had failed to control the behaviour of Telmex, still the country's dominant provider of telecommunications. Telmex had been illegitimately preventing other companies from using the established network to offer competing long-distance telephone services. Telmex had allegedly failed to offer interconnection services to other suppliers at reasonable rates, making access to Mexican consumers commercially impossible. In 2004, the WTO panel issued its judgment, ruling that Mexico had failed to ensure reasonable non-discriminatory market access to and use of existing telecommunications networks operated by Telmex. Remember that the WTO cannot take action against private companies directly – only against governments. Failing to control Telmex's behaviour was contrary to Mexico's specific commitments under GATS (national treatment and market access). The panel said that Mexico should have ensured that services providers from other countries like the US, as well as several Latin American countries that were interested in getting in on the Mexican telecommunications industry, were able to connect to the existing network at a cost-oriented (not expensive) fee. The panel disagreed with Mexico's argument that in order to be granted access to the Mexican market, foreign companies should have been required to contribute to the enhancement of the country's telecommunications infrastructure, which was something Mexico needed as a developing country. The Telmex case has been criticized for failing to accord WTO members sufficient 'policy space' to develop their own economies. In the case of Mexico, not yet a full market economy, this might mean that some industries were not yet able to face full-scale competition, as they would be in the more advanced American situation. Mexico ultimately complied with the ruling by establishing regulations allowing for the commercial sale of long-distance services originating in Mexico, effectively allowing foreign suppliers to compete on an equal footing with the giant Telmex. This didn't seem to faze Slim, whose share of Telmex, which remains the dominant fixed-line telecommunications provider in Mexico, has continued to rise in value. In 2013, Forbes reported that Slim, with personal wealth of more than US $71 billion, had held on to his title as the richest person in the world for a third year in a row, just ahead of Bill Gates. Clearly competition sometimes means that the strong get stronger.

Some particular services sectors are considered to be so economically important that they deserved special attention under the GATS. Simply listing commitments in these sectors wasn't enough. Instead the GATS has four annexes, which are essentially additional optional commitments that can be accepted by WTO members on very important and highly contentious spheres of economic activity in services.

The annex on the movement of natural persons deals with negotiations on the rights of people to stay temporarily in a country for the purpose of providing a service, essentially an elaboration of the Mode 4 movement of natural persons mode of services delivery. As with Mode 4, this annex doesn't apply to conditions for citizenship, permanent residence or permanent employment. The annex on financial services was drawn up because of the understanding that instability in the banking sector has the potential to undermine the whole economy, which it very nearly did in the recent global financial crisis. This supplement to the GATS allows governments to take prudential measures to ensure the integrity of the financial system, including provisions relating to the protection of investors, depositors and insurance policyholders. Allowing member countries to enact such laws was largely ineffectual in dealing with the recent economic crisis, but carving out national policy space for these precautions may prove crucial in the future, in light of the new-found aversion to risk in banking. The financial services annex also excludes services provided by central banks when exercising their governmental authority over the financial system. There is also an annex on telecommunications which specifies that governments must ensure that foreign service providers are given access to the existing telecommunications network without discrimination, which was also relevant to the Mexico telecoms dispute discussed above. This guarantee recognizes the importance of telecommunications to many other spheres of services activity, such as legal advice given over the phone as well as electronic transfers of money. Finally, under the annex on air transport services, multimillion dollar air traffic rights and directly related activities are excluded from GATS coverage. The GATS does apply to aircraft repair and maintenance services as well as marketing of airlines.

As I mentioned above, efforts continue to liberalize services further under the GATS as part of the Doha Round of WTO trade negotiations. The first stage of negotiations ended successfully in 2001 when WTO members agreed on the procedures for the negotiations themselves, paving the way for further substantial commitments in the future. The first phase of negotiations also endorsed some of the GATS' fundamental principles, including the right of members to regulate their own services economies and to introduce new regulations on the supply of services in the pursuit of national economic policy objectives. Since 2002 a process of bilateral negotiations on market access has been taking place, guided by these central principles. Ongoing negotiations for services liberalization in the Doha Round have not been as successful as many would have liked them to be, especially multinational firms seeking new markets. But there have been some major achievements, especially in opening key services like banking and telecommunications in some of the large emerging markets like China and India. Russia also made encouraging commitments under GATS as part of its accession package.

It should be stressed that Doha Round services negotiations take place essentially on a bilateral basis, with members outlining ways in which they can improve their specific commitments on market access and national treatment in order to ensure that privileges given to local companies are also given to foreign companies. In late 2014, during preliminary discussions on the future of services negotiations, WTO members acknowledged that it would be difficult to make substantial gains on deeper services liberalization without progress in agricultural subsidies. This reflects the interrelatedness of all forms of trade negotiations – persistent faltering in agriculture has the potential to unravel success in spheres like banking and transportation. Various techniques for improving negotiations were also discussed, including holding informal debates and a focus on realistic and achievable goals.

Again, at the heart of WTO rules we see the preservation of individual country autonomy. Without this crucial foundation, seen also in the selective, optional commitments for national treatment and market access under the GATS, there likely would have been no coverage of services under the WTO at all. And even where commitments have been made, these are still subject to the General Exceptions for public policy concerns discussed in the previous chapter, such as those relating to culture and morals, as well as traditional governmental services like education and health care.

Despite the existence of annexes on the opening up of telecommunications and financial services, it is a mistake to suggest that GATS directly regulates monopolies or anti-competitive behaviour, although it does contain some rules on monopolization of services. GATS does require that members ensure that any monopoly service providers do not violate commitments under GATS regarding market access and non-discrimination, but it does not say anywhere that monopolies are prohibited. This is up to each country's own rules on competition (or antitrust as it is known in the US). If a company becomes so powerful that it is damaging a market by distorting prices, this may be illegal under many countries' laws (as it is in the EU and the US, for example) but this is itself not a violation of the GATS, and the WTO has no competency to deal with market abuse through dominance. Many countries are quite content with monopolies; in fact, some of these companies are themselves owned by the state, as is the case in China, Russia and some Latin American countries. The fact remains, however, that market dominance in the form of a monopoly may lead to transgression of a member's GATS commitments, in which case the member must take action to curtail this behaviour. If it does not, and this results in a GATS violation, then the WTO dispute settlement procedure may be engaged.

While GATS ensures that foreign suppliers of services in listed sectors do not suffer discrimination, and that the sectors in which they operate are not subject to restrictions on market access, it is not intended to compensate companies from other countries for any difficulties they might face from consumers because they are foreign. Some of us just naturally prefer to use suppliers we are familiar with because, well, maybe we just don't like foreigners. The 'liability of foreignness' is a natural feature of the market. In the UK, for example, the broadband supplier Plusnet emphasizes its roots in Yorkshire in order to appeal to British customers' sense of national pride or the perception that a local company will understand their needs more. Some people might even be willing to pay more to get a service from a local company. GATS can't do anything about this as long as such favouritism is not fostered by the government.

Some further competency for the WTO in the field of competition law has been recommended by a number of prominent commentators. This type of enlargement seems to make sense, given that the cross-border component of many multinationals' activities may end up resulting in abuse of a dominant position within a series of national or international markets. As I mentioned in chapter 3, the WTO's dispute settlement system in particular has been identified as a suitable 'world court' of international competition law. But, of course, given that the WTO cannot enforce any rules against private companies, only against their governments, this expansion of the WTO's role from trade into competition would require a complete rewriting of the organization's scope and mandate, and this is highly unlikely. With goods, services and, as we will see in chapter 8, intellectual property, the WTO already has quite enough on its plate.

In the next chapter we will see how the WTO has gone even further to allow member states to regulate in the sphere of health and safety for all kinds of traded goods, while attempting to ensure that these manifestations of national policy are not used as a way to sneak in disguised protectionism.

7

Health and safety: food and product standards as barriers to trade

One of the most vital concerns of any government is the health of its people and, by extension, the safety of the foods and other products that its consumers use. Ensuring that citizens are supplied with food that is not harmful to them, and products that are safe, can be problematic from the standpoint of trade because one country might have a very different view to another of what constitutes safety or health. Similarly, as with any sphere of domestic regulation, there is a risk that a government may attempt to justify health and safety standards on goods as an underhanded way of protecting domestic producers.

The WTO addresses this dilemma by according member countries the right to regulate in the interests of health and safety as they wish, but requiring them to provide evidence of the dangers associated with failing to do so. In this way it balances the sovereignty of nations, in their legitimate attempts to safeguard their citizens, against the goal of free trade among nations. Health and safety standards must not be used in a manner that operates as a covert restriction on international trade, meaning where there is no authentic, demonstrable reason for them. As you can imagine, like many spheres of WTO rules, this can be quite controversial. At what point does a particular food become unsafe for human consumption so that you can restrict its entry into your country? When exactly does a certain product become harmful? How dangerous does it have to be to health for it to be banned, or subject to some kind of onerous testing?

The WTO attempts to answer these questions through two key systems of rules, the unfortunately named Agreement on Sanitary and Phytosanitary measures (SPS) and the Agreement on Technical Barriers to Trade (TBT). Together these sets of rules require WTO member countries to use scientific evidence or international standards when setting food and general product safety laws. These obligations help prevent member countries from creating artificial barriers to trade in the form of onerous product standards, such as those involving laboratory testing and labelling. The SPS and TBT agreements are examples of the WTO's efforts towards what is sometimes called 'positive harmonization'. This means that the WTO establishes minimum standards that its member countries must follow when enacting health and safety laws. 'Positive' indicates that these are areas where the WTO tells its members what they must do (e.g. health regulations must be based on scientific evidence), not what they must *not* do, as it does for example under the GATT (e.g. do *not* impose quantitative restrictions). 'Harmonization' simply means that the WTO wants all of its countries to adopt similar rules in order to minimize the cost borne by traders in adapting their goods to fit each national market to which they export. One size fits all is better than made to measure when it comes to health and safety laws.

As liberalization of barriers to trade has progressed, the regulation of health and safety standards has become an increasing source of tension. This trend is tied to the expansion of the 'regulatory state', which some liken to an intrusive 'nanny state' that the West has experienced since the middle of the twentieth century. Compliance with an ever-increasing number of rules intended to protect us from scary things is especially hard for developing countries that lack the resources to screen and test the products they export to us hypersensitive people in rich countries. Importing countries in the developed world are just as likely to complain that weak standards in countries of origin can create health and safety risks for their own citizens. They also constitute an unfair trade advantage because of lower compliance costs. Meanwhile civil society groups tend to emphasize that governments are democratically accountable to ensure that citizens are not harmed by the goods they consume. As usual, the WTO is stuck in the middle.

Health regulations

Given the importance of safety standards for food, the WTO decided to create a special agreement for food safety and animal and plant health standards. This is the Sanitary and Phytosanitary Measures (SPS) Agreement. Phytosanitary simply means the health of plants. This agreement allows countries to set their own standards in relation to food, animal and plant health. However, in order for these rules to be viewed as legitimate by the WTO from the standpoint of their effect on international trade, they must be justified either through science or through deference to a recognized international standard-setting body. The SPS lists three such organizations (the awkwardly named Codex Alimentarius Commission, Office International des Epizooties, and Secretariat of the International Plant Protection Convention), none of which has a direct relationship with the WTO itself.

WTO members are therefore encouraged to implement international standards, guidelines and recommendations on food safety, where they exist. Rules which conform to international standards are presumed to conform to the SPS. If these guidelines do exist and WTO members adhere to them, then it is unlikely that such regulations would ever lead to a dispute because of this built-in assumption that they are valid.

One of the foundational principles of the SPS is that, provided there is scientific justification, WTO members are permitted to enact laws that result in higher standards than those indicated by international bodies. This means that there must be adequate risk assessment of the dangers to human, animal or plant life or health. Adequate risk assessment will likely include having scientists examine the relevant products for various diseases and organisms, testing the likelihood of citizens being exposed to them under different conditions, and what the actual dangers are in terms of shortening of life spans, and so on. If there is insufficient scientific evidence to demonstrate that a particular health regulation is needed, for example, a certain quarantine period for a type of fish before it can be frozen, WTO member countries may provisionally adopt the law anyway on the basis of the available pertinent information. This is a kind of risk-averse, 'best guess' approach, but it does require that the country make an effort to seek the additional information in order to get a more complete picture later on.

The SPS Agreement also says that countries should only apply food health regulations to the extent necessary to protect human, animal and plant life or health. This means that there must not be a less trade-restrictive way to achieve the same goal, taking into account technical and economic feasibility. Further, members should not arbitrarily or unjustifiably discriminate between countries where identical or similar conditions prevail. So, you should not prohibit a certain type of apple from one country but not from a second country, where the apples in both countries have the same likelihood of exposure to dangerous organisms. This is basically what the US did in the shrimp case and what the EU did in the seals case.

Food health standards can be set based on an appropriate assessment of risk as long as the approach taken to assess the risk is consistent and not arbitrary. In this sense it is very much about the process of risk evaluation, rather than the actual outcome in terms of specific levels of chemicals, and so on.

The SPS has attracted quite a bit of attention from the WTO courts, particularly in recent years. Shortly after the creation of the WTO in the mid-1990s, Canada brought a claim against Australia on the basis of an alleged violation of the SPS because of Australia's particular rules relating to imports of salmon. Australia imposed quarantine on salmon imports from Canada because of dangers that this fish could pose to the health of its consumers. Canada argued that this violated the SPS because the risk assessment which formed the basis of the quarantine law was arbitrary – it applied only to salmon that was consumer-ready (meaning fresh from the ocean), without any justification of why that particular type of salmon was more dangerous than other types and in what way. Ruling in favour of Canada, the Appellate Body determined that distinctions in the level of protection required (consumer-ready and non-consumer-ready) were not justified because the risk was equally high in the two different situations. Essentially there was no scientific basis for the imposition of different quarantine standards for two different types of the same fish. Or, put another way, the quarantine requirement was more trade-restrictive than required to safeguard the health of Australian consumers.

The most famous dispute to have arisen in conjunction with the SPS is still probably the beef hormone case brought by the US and others, against the European Union. Hormone-treated beef is still controversial, as many people are worried about ingesting animal products that have been treated with any kind of chemicals, especially growth hormones intended to cause animals to gain weight before they are slaughtered. It seems that Europeans are more worried about this type of thing than people in America, where there is a long tradition of processing meat into things like hamburgers and hot dogs. If you've ever eaten a hamburger at a restaurant in the US, chances are you've eaten hormone-treated beef. Not that you would notice – if done properly, the amount of hormones added is so slight that they are many thousands of times less than what humans produce normally themselves.

Because of European sensitivities in this area, the European Union imposed a ban on the sale of beef from animals that had been treated with growth hormones. While the ban had almost no effect on European beef producers, it inflicted serious damage on US beef producers, who either could not sell their product in Europe or had to take expensive measures to ensure that it was hormone-free. Bringing its grievance to the WTO courts, the US argued that the ban was disguised protectionism in favour of European beef suppliers, whereas the European Union said that the ban was a legitimate public health measure designed to protect its citizens from the possible health risks linked to hormones in beef. The Appellate Body ended up siding with the US, because the EU's regulatory measures in favour of health did not conform to international standards – there was no international guideline specifying the dangers of hormones in beef. Further, the European standards were not based on a clear scientifically based risk assessment; they essentially reflected cultural tastes more than anything else. So, the WTO was essentially saying that the Europeans' fear of hormones was idiosyncratic and unjustified. Hormone-treated beef could be sold in Europe.

In reaching this conclusion, the WTO courts clarified that some minimum level of risk assessment must be conducted in order to justify a regulation, even if it fell short of establishing clear and irrefutable evidence. In that sense, the WTO does accord members significant freedom to enact the food health laws that they want for the reasons that they want, as long as there is some indication of integrity in the process, which was absent in Europe's control of the alleged risks associated with hormone-treated beef. The Appellate Body went even further in allowing discretion to members in relation to their SPS rules when it said that the presence of a 'scientific controversy' or disagreement about a particular health danger does not prevent a country from relying upon minority scientific opinion, as opposed to the mainstream. Of course, minority scientific opinion cannot rely on the rantings of an amateur spouting conspiracy theory – it must come from 'qualified and respected sources', whatever that means. It seems that the controversy boils down to the question of what exactly constitutes science, and it is not clear that anyone has that answer.

It should also be noted that unravelling the specific risks in relation to certain products is particularly problematic for the WTO courts, where much of the evidence upon which risk assessment is based is in the hands of the private producers of dangerous products, not the governments themselves which come before the WTO as negotiators and litigators.

THE PRECAUTIONARY PRINCIPLE

Governments can be so worried about a particular risk to the health of their citizens that they are willing to impose laws without having any genuine scientific or even rational basis for doing so. This reflects the reality that, as humans or, more cynically, as voters, we are sometimes afraid of things that aren't really there. Flesh-eating zombies or alien invaders are fairly obviously nonsensical fears, even if they thrill moviegoers. Whether global warming or antibi- otic-resistant superbugs are matters of genuine concern for human- ity is less clear, at least to some sceptics. Mindful that they need to be responsive to their citizens, governments often invoke what is known as the Precautionary Principle, which essentially embodies the logic of 'better safe than sorry'. Instead of waiting until a risk is proven, at which point someone has usually been hurt or killed, a law is passed that prevents the dangerous activity before anything happens. This often means that the law is unnecessary, or overly risk-averse, which in turn usually means that too much money has been spent on a safety precaution, or in the case of international trade, a product that wasn't actually unsafe gets banned, 'just in case' someone, somewhere might possibly have been hurt by it. While the Precautionary Principle can satisfy people's irrational fears, whether it is about microscopic organisms or flesh-eating zombies, it is problematically overcautious to some people, because by definition the Precautionary Principle means that there is not yet enough empirical data to support the ban or prohibition. In the beef hormones dispute, the Appellate Body stopped short of declaring that the Precautionary Principle has evolved into a principle of international law, but it did observe that the SPS Agreement allows countries to adopt provisional measures in the absence of scientific evidence to conduct risk assessment, and that countries are entitled to establish their own levels of sanitary protection. This permits governments to act from the perspective of prudence and caution where risks of irreversible damage to human life are involved. In allowing countries to adopt the Precautionary Principle when setting their SPS rules, the Appellate Body memorably said that when considering danger to human life: 'the risk to be evaluated is not only risk ascertainable in a science laboratory operating under strictly controlled conditions, but also risk in human societies as they actually exist, in other words, the actual potential for adverse effects on human health in the real world where people live and work and die'. This common sense approach is perhaps the best way of balancing the risk of doing something against the risk of not doing it.

The SPS was argued in the WTO courts again in another very controversial dispute relating to genetically modified organisms (GMOs). GMOs are organic products created through gene manipulation by companies, notably Monsanto in the US, to be superior to naturally occurring equivalents, often because they are resistant to insects or can grow larger or in less hospitable environments. GMOs are seen by many as a vital tool in the eradication of world hunger. Others view them as a dangerous interference with Mother Nature, potentially leading to disastrous consequences for human, animal and plant ecosystems as well as the private property of more traditional farmers. In the GMO dispute at the WTO, the US, as well as Canada and Argentina, challenged the European Union's regulatory regime for the approval of GMOs, which led to unacceptable delays for genetically modified foods entering the European market. In a judgment that ran to almost a thousand pages, the panel ruled that some of the EU's bans on certain GMO crops did not satisfy the requirements of the SPS – although members are permitted to adopt temporary measures while they are engaging in scientific research to get a more complete picture, some of the studies carried out by the EU up to that point had in fact showed that the GMO foods were safe. The panel saw these as sufficient risk assessments which demonstrated that the bans were not legitimate, and therefore had to be removed. Europe complied with this ruling, although to this day Austria still maintains some bans on genetically modified maize, in defiance of the WTO. Some countries also require that genetically modified food be labelled as such.

The GMO case again illustrates the WTO's emphasis on process rather than on results as a way of resolving an incredibly sensitive dispute between two superpowers. The WTO doesn't want to depict itself as the final arbiter of scientific truth in tightly contested disputes, but rather as a body that scrutinizes the way in which any governmental decisions that have effects on trade are reached. It seems that the highly complex way in which the EU makes these types of decisions may be at the core of the GMO debate rather than anything fundamental about the relative safety of GMO and natural foods. Negotiations on the way in which each individual EU member state deals with GMO foods originating from the US and other countries continue to languish within the EU's bureaucratic framework. If the EU were able to allow each of its constituent states to establish its own rules on safety and therefore trade of GMOs, rather than having to satisfy all of its twenty-seven members' wishes as a federal entity, then there may have been a more even-handed way of controlling the entry of GMO products to the satisfaction of both sides.

Safety regulations

Like health, regulations relating to product safety and other technical requirements, like those dealing with environmental protection and consumer welfare laws, can be as important for safeguarding the citizens of WTO member countries. Problems arise when there are too many different standards across the world. This is because it is difficult for the producers and exporters of goods not only to comply with these rules but sometimes even to know what they are in the first place. Ironically, some technical regulations actually have the purpose of enhancing trade by informing consumers precisely where products originate from and what they contain. As with health-related rules, technical regulations of all sorts can become instruments of protectionism – they can be used as obstacles to international trade by imposing entirely unnecessary or overly complicated procedures on exporters. The job of the WTO is to ensure that technical regulations are genuine.

The Technical Barriers to Trade (TBT) Agreement attempts to ensure that regulations and standards as well as testing and certification procedures do not create illegitimate barriers to international trade under the guise of safety or consumer protection. It obliges WTO members not to enact technical regulations that are more trade-restrictive than necessary in order to fulfil the legitimate objective. When assessing this, the member country must consider the risks that non-fulfilment of the policy goal, for example consumer safety, would impose on its people. This essentially means that the efforts undertaken by each country in achieving a particular product safety or consumer awareness objective must be done in a manner that does not restrict international trade. So, any such laws must be clearly connected to the risk that is being controlled. The more serious the risk, the greater an imposition on international trade permissible.

Discrimination against other WTO members is prohibited under the TBT. Members are required to accord imported products treatment that is no less favourable than 'like' domestic products, a concept that is quite familiar to us from GATT. In the context of the TBT, likeness will mean that the products are in a competitive relationship with one another. This means that differential treatment results in a distortion of the marketplace – products end up being more expensive or harder to get than they should be because of the unequal nature of the technical regulation. The safety risks that are being pursued by national governments will also be relevant when assessing likeness under the TBT. The agreement does acknowledge a country's entitlement to use the standards that it considers appropriate for various forms of protection, such as citizens' safety, environmental protection or consumer needs. Again this reflects the WTO's deference to the will of its members – they are free to impose the regulations they want based on their own concerns for the health and safety of their citizens.

In order to deal with the problem of confusion between many complex, overlapping regulations instigated by each of the WTO's members, the TBT Agreement encourages governments to adopt international standards where they can – the idea being that international standards will be understood and recognized by many more countries, cutting through much of the red tape. Unlike the SPS Agreement, however, the TBT does not prescribe any specific international standard-setting bodies. This is because the TBT has much broader coverage than the SPS, so there are far too many standard-setting bodies that would need to be considered. The international standards for the TBT can come from a wide range of sources, most notably regulatory within each domestic government. For example, standards relating to electrical appliances for sale and use in Europe are reviewed by the European Committee for Standardization, which is part of the European Commission, a governmental department of the European Union. The European Committee for Standardization ensures that standards initially established by national governments are effectively equivalent to those in other European countries.

The TBT sets out a code of good practice for governments as well as industry bodies to prepare and adopt voluntary standards. As you know, the WTO has no direct control over non-governmental organizations like companies or industry groups. But this does not stop it from trying to encourage these groups to standardize their rules in order to eliminate some of the complications surrounding multiple playbooks. In keeping with the WTO's overarching principle of transparency and openness, the TBT instructs members to publish all of their regulations in as accessible a format as possible.

Under the TBT, WTO members are told to design their regulations based on product requirements in terms of their performance, meaning how they work, rather than design or description, meaning what goes into them. Regulations must be tied to the aspects of the good that can actually be harmful, such as rules on testing of kettles in order to prevent electric shocks, not rules based on colour or the type of plastic used, unless these could somehow be relevant to the product's safety.

There have been a number of disputes between WTO members on the basis of the TBT Agreement, although the total is still somewhat less than under the SPS Agreement. In recent years the TBT Agreement has become more widely used by WTO members, in part because of the explosion of safety rules for all sorts of products, many of which could be exploited as potential barriers to trade in an era of declining tariffs. One of the first major battles fought under the TBT dealt with another fish – this time sardines.

Sardines are a bit like Marmite; you either love them or hate them. Whether or not they are part of your diet, it's fairly certain that you at least know what a sardine is when you see it or taste it (or smell it). We all know that sardines are a type of oily, salty fish that you get from cans and put on sandwiches, or sometimes on a plate if you want to be fancy. But the word 'sardine' actually originated with a type of fish caught off the island of Sardinia in the Mediterranean Sea. Does that mean true 'sardines' must come from the waters around that island? Peru didn't think so, and it was prepared to go to the WTO over it. In 2001, Peru challenged a European regulation that only food products prepared from a certain subspecies of sardines found around the coasts of the eastern North Atlantic Ocean as well as the Mediterranean and Black Seas could be marketed as 'sardines'. Only products of this species could be sold on the shelves of European stores with the word 'sardines' on the tin. Obviously this was a problem for Peru as it is on the other side of the world and therefore could never produce 'sardines' from its waters.

Peru argued that the European regulation violated the TBT because it did not adhere to international standards set by the Codex Alimentarius Commission, one of the organizations that the WTO views as having the presumed authority to set standards relating to product safety. The Commission said that the label 'sardines' was not restricted to species of fish found in the North Atlantic, Mediterranean and Black Sea. The WTO panel, and later the Appellate Body, agreed with Peru, ruling that the international standard limited the sardines to various species (which included those kinds found in the waters around Peru) and that this international standard was effective in accomplishing all three of Europe's objectives in their tighter regulation: market transparency, consumer protection and fair competition. Europe's restriction on the definition of sardines was nothing more than an attempt to promote the sale of European fish.

Another important instigation of the TBT came about in relation to the French prohibition on the importation or sale of asbestos products. In 2000, this law was challenged by Canada, which has a major asbestos production industry, mostly concentrated in the French-speaking province of Quebec. Asbestos, a material composed of thin fibrous crystals, was widely used throughout the nineteenth and twentieth centuries because of its resistance to heat as well as its affordability. Many industrial buildings from that period (including my university office before it was renovated) used asbestos insulation inside external walls, but the prolonged inhalation of asbestos fibres can cause lung damage and even cancer. In the dispute brought by Canada against the EU, the challenged law was both the ban on Canadian asbestos as well as exceptions to it for certain types of cellulose and glass fibres. Unfortunately, while the Appellate Body stated that the TBT Agreement was relevant to the dispute, it declined to rule one way or the other how that agreement should be applied to the case, deciding the issue in favour of France on the basis of GATT's national treatment rule (specifically by allowing France to apply the prohibition on Canadian asbestos based on GATT's health exception). The somewhat frustrating lack of discussion on the TBT Agreement, despite its clear relevance, is an example of what lawyers call judicial economy – basically the court attempts to avoid making any rulings that it does not have to if there's an easier way to reach a decision. In the court's mind it was easier to use GATT national treatment, with its decades of established jurisprudence, than the relatively untested TBT Agreement.

The relevance of the asbestos case to what we are talking about in this chapter can be found in the WTO courts' useful explanation of the reach of the TBT agreement. In this dispute the panel and Appellate Body laid out what constitutes a technical regulation such that it is captured by the TBT. Technical regulations will consist of mandatory requirements relating to a product's characteristics, which can be by physical descriptions as well as functionality. This definition, which the Appellate Body thought fit the EU's asbestos ban, is now regularly cited in WTO disputes whenever technical regulations are challenged. It means that the TBT agreement is often engaged when the GATT's General Exceptions relating to health and safety on all kinds of products (other than food, which is the domain of the SPS Agreement) are used as a justification for an otherwise trade-restrictive regime. Indeed the TBT Agreement (as well as the SPSP Agreement) is often described as an enlargement of the more general language contained in the GATT General Exceptions. WTO courts often will examine a challenged regulation from the perspective of both regimes.

One of the most interesting recent uses of the TBT involved Indonesia's 2010 complaint against the US because of the US's prohibition on clove-flavoured cigarettes. The US domestic law of 2009 banned the production or sale of cigarettes containing the additive clove (as well as other flavourings like cherry, vanilla and coconut) but expressly allowed the production and sale of cigarettes containing other additives, such as the popular flavouring menthol, almost all of which were produced in the US. The reason for the restriction on these varieties of flavoured cigarettes was to ensure that young people, who were seen as being more likely to be attracted by the same types of flavouring found in sweets, would not become hooked on cigarettes and thus become lifetime smokers. Indonesia, which is the world's leading producer of clove cigarettes, argued that this law violated national treatment under the GATT as well as the TBT and the SPS Agreements. The WTO panel agreed, basing their finding on the fact that clove cigarettes are 'like' menthol cigarettes because they appeal to young smokers. When the US appealed the decision, the Appellate Body agreed with most of the panel's conclusions, adding that the US law had a severe detrimental impact on the competitive opportunities of Indonesia's clove cigarettes, which was a critical component of the non-discrimination guarantee in the TBT. At the time of writing this book, the US has still not complied with the rulings of the WTO courts. While not removing its ban on clove or other flavoured cigarettes in order to comply with the WTO courts' ruling on TBT compliance, the US has indicated that it intends to pursue further studies in relation to menthol and may ultimately impose restrictions on the use of this type of flavouring in tobacco products.

In 2013, Indonesia got stroppy again over its cigarette exports, this time over Australia's plain-packaging requirements. Four previous disputes have been launched against Australia over these rules, initiated by the major tobacco producers Honduras, Ukraine, the Dominican Republic and Cuba. Many other WTO members have joined the proceedings against Australia. The complaining countries argue that the plain-packaging laws violate Australia's commitments under the TBT (discrimination and unnecessary restrictions on trade) as well as under the WTO's intellectual property agreement, which we will explore in the next chapter. At the time of writing, this dispute is at the stage of consultation, and the establishment of a panel is pending. Plain-packaging laws require that cigarette packaging must not display any branding, such as colours or logos. Manufacturers may only print the brand name in ordinary, non-stylized letters, in addition to any mandatory health warnings required by local laws. All tobacco products therefore appear in standardized, usually plain brown packaging. While many countries have debated whether or not to impose plain-packaging rules for cigarettes, Australia was the first country in the world actually to implement them, with its Tobacco Plain Packaging Act of 2011. The logic behind the scheme is that smokers tend to be highly influenced by the design and presentation of cigarettes in their packages, and as such it is anticipated that smoking will decline because of the unappealing, nondescript wrapping. Numerous studies conducted in Australia and elsewhere, which I imagine will ultimately feature in the WTO panel proceedings once they get under way, have indicated that people are more likely to quit smoking or to smoke less when they are presented with cigarettes in plain packages. This trend appears to be particularly strong in younger smokers, who choose to smoke or not to smoke for the rest of their lives during their teens.

Unsurprisingly, the tobacco companies have strongly resisted plain packaging. In fact, the tobacco company Philip Morris brought a claim directly against Australia under the Australia–Hong Kong bilateral investment treaty (which gives companies a direct route to bringing legal action against countries, unlike

the WTO system). That dispute, which is based on the argument
that there are no legitimate health benefits associated with plain
packaging and as such the laws are an affront to the commercial
freedom of foreign investors, has not yet been resolved. Should
the complaints initiated by Indonesia and other countries against
Australia reach the level of a full WTO dispute, the panel will
have to scrutinize the extent to which Australia's plain-packaging
law has an illegitimate effect on trade, meaning that it represents
an unnecessary barrier to foreign cigarettes vis-à-vis Australian
cigarettes without sufficient health justification. The outcome of
this dispute might turn on how the sales of Australian-produced
cigarettes have been affected by the rule relative to their foreign
counterparts. There are numerous other ongoing lawsuits, many
of which are proceeding in domestic courts, over restrictions on
tobacco marketing, which has been heavily regulated across most
of the developed world since the 1970s. Some of the tension
appears to be the result of the developing world's lag in terms of
the social acceptability of smoking. It should be mentioned that
the plain cigarette packaging dispute raises important additional
issues relating to the protection of intellectual property. In
particular, requiring tobacco companies to use plain packages
can be seen as an infringement on their right to use their trademarks, potentially engaging the WTO's Trade Related Aspects
of Intellectual Property (TRIPS) Agreement. The WTO's treatment of intellectual property will be considered in more detail
in the next chapter.

Clearly the right to protect the health of young people from
the dangers of tobacco addiction is a key aspect of any government's duty towards its citizens, and one that should arguably
trump its obligations to unimpeded international trade. In the
clove cigarettes dispute, the WTO showed that the US ban
appeared ultimately to be motivated more by the goal of preserving the profits of US tobacco companies that produce menthol
cigarettes, which may well be just as dangerous as clove-flavoured

ones coming from other countries. It is precisely this kind of abuse of health and safety regulations that bothers the WTO. It's a tough call as to whether there is really protectionism going on in these types of cases, and the WTO's reputation takes a beating if it gets it wrong, which of course is often a matter of opinion.

The SPS and TBT disputes show one of the most fascinating qualities of the WTO as an institution of global governance. Instead of coming down heavy-handedly on countries for pursuing regulatory policies in relation to very sensitive, health-related matters like genetically modified food and cigarettes, matters that most would agree should fall within the sphere of democratically elected national governments, the WTO instead has kept true to its own narrow mandate of trade. The WTO does not dictate that we should not smoke or that we should eat hormone-treated beef, nor has it declared that these things are unhealthy or not. What it has done is look at the unnecessary distortions of international trade caused by legitimate health-oriented laws that could have been imposed in a less arbitrary manner and had a smaller effect on world markets. The WTO tells us that health regulations are within the sphere of national governments, but artificial barriers to trade posing as health policy are not.

8
Keeping it real: the protection of intellectual property rights

Protecting intellectual property is a vital component of the global economy, particularly in high-technology sectors such as pharmaceuticals and because of the rise of the Internet, which has allowed instantaneous copying of lucrative art forms like music and movies. The global market for illegally copied goods and services moving through international trade is thought to be worth more than US $250 billion per year.

During the early 1990s, in the period leading up to the creation of the WTO, concerns in the US and other major developed countries intensified over the loss of valuable exports in newly industrializing markets due to counterfeiting, which was itself the result of weak or non-existent intellectual property laws. Developed countries were worried that they were losing their competitive advantage in the production of high-value-added goods and services to poorer countries that had acquired the capacity to copy these goods at low cost. Bringing intellectual property protection into the regime of the new WTO became a top priority and the focus of extensive lobbying efforts by US, Japanese and European multinationals.

The rationale for protecting intellectual property is both moral and economic. It is only right that hard-working, creative people should be rewarded for their skill and effort. Even more so when this brings pleasure or improves the lives of others.

More practically speaking, where intellectual property rights are not protected, this reduces the incentive for innovation, which in the long term can be problematic because we all want to be able to enjoy new inventions and works of art. Still, critics of these laws point out that it is simply not believable that weak intellectual property protection reduces these incentives, at least in the context of international trade, because insufficient disposable income in poor countries means that they are not really significant markets for intellectual property. Moreover, these countries lack the technological capacity to reproduce many of the most advanced forms of intellectual property, such as those protected by patents, so they shouldn't really be seen as a threat. These claims have led some commentators to suggest that the WTO should never have concerned itself with intellectual property at all.

The WTO protects international trade in intellectual property through one instrument: the Agreement on Trade-Related Aspects of Intellectual Property Rights or TRIPS. The basis of the TRIPS is the familiar concept of non-discrimination that we've seen in GATT and GATS. Member states of the WTO promise to treat their own nationals and foreigners equally with respect to obtaining and protecting intellectual property rights, just as they must treat nationals from all other countries the same. As with the other agreements, this commitment ensures that the trading companies do not get advantages on the basis of where they come from. This controls distortions in the international market for innovative or original goods and services.

TRIPS: common ground rules

In addition to the umbrella principle of equality among intellectual property rights holders, the TRIPS sets minimum levels of protection for various forms of intellectual property that must be provided under the national laws of each member country. WTO members must ensure that their national legislation on each of the major recognized forms of intellectual property conforms to these baseline requirements. If it does not, then other member countries can bring claims through the WTO dispute settlement system on that basis. As we've seen earlier, the companies that own the intellectual property rights have no standing on their own to appear before the WTO courts.

The minimum standards of protection for the chief forms of intellectual property are drawn from earlier international treaties like the Paris Convention and the Berne Convention, which themselves are founded on common understandings of what constitutes intellectual property in the legal systems of the developed world. In that sense, there isn't anything very new about TRIPS. The TRIPS Agreement is another example of what international lawyers call 'positive harmonization' – the attempt to ensure that each country in the world adopts the same type of standards within its national laws, not by imposing one set of laws directly at the international level. This is one way that the WTO helps establish a system of globally applicable rules without infringing too much on each country's ability to govern itself. While member states must adopt the minimum level of protection indicated by the WTO, they are free to impose stronger protections, just as they have some room to apply the protections in the manner that they wish.

In order to get a sense of how TRIPS works, it's important to understand what intellectual property law actually is. The first category of intellectual property covered by the TRIPS Agreement is copyright. TRIPS specifies that copyright is only extended to the expression of an idea, not the idea itself. This is how copyright is commonly understood in intellectual property law systems around the world. The agreement then sets out that the holders of copyright (e.g. authors of books, composers of songs, and other types of creative artists including those who own computer programs and databases) must have the right to prevent the unauthorized reproduction of their work for at least fifty years after their death. So, fifty years after the author of a work dies, it falls into the public domain, meaning that it can be reproduced without the payment of any royalties to the author's estate. This is how companies like Amazon can give out free electronic copies of old books like Shakespeare's plays and Sherlock Holmes stories with their Kindles – they are allowed to copy and distribute them en masse for free. The authors have been dead for a sufficiently long time that the law deems enough profit has been made from their work and the public should therefore be able to enjoy it for free. Some organizations, like Project Gutenberg (named after the inventor of the first printing press), are assembling an online database of books that have fallen into public domain based on the fifty-year post-death rule. You can download these old works for free legally. There are some exceptions to the fifty-year post-death rule, where the prohibition on reproduction is extended for up to fifty years after the making of the copyrighted work, notably cinematographic works (movies), which are protected for twenty-five years after making. It is worth noting that some countries, like the UK, have stronger protections, applying copy-right protection for seventy years after the death of the author. Remember that the TRIPS sets minimum, not maximum stand-ards of protection of intellectual property rights.

Free reproduction of copyrighted works outside these time limits is permitted by TRIPS when the works are reproduced for teaching purposes or for reporting on current events. The rationale behind these exceptions, which again are found in most national intellectual property law systems around the world, as well as in international treaties like the Berne Convention, is that it is in the public interest to encourage the use of artistic works for educational purposes and to disseminate knowledge in a non-commercial context. But in order for those who reproduce copy-righted works to fall within these exceptions, they must show that they have not caused an unreasonable loss of income to the copyright holder. This is the reason that you often see warnings near photocopiers in libraries stating that you should not reproduce all of a book, but only the chapters or pages you need for your personal use as a student or teacher. The same rules apply to electronic copying or downloading.

TRIPS provisions on the limits of copyright came under investigation by the WTO dispute settlement system in a complaint brought by Europe against the US relating to the playing of music in public places. Many bars and restaurants, coffee shops and other types of retail establishments play background music to their customers, sometimes off the radio or sometimes prerecorded playlists or streamed from the Internet using websites like Spotify. If you were cynical, you might be tempted to argue that these commercial premises are stealing music in order to encourage customers to stay and buy things. Indeed this was the essence of Europe's complaint at the WTO. Under US domestic copyright law, as in many countries, use of music in stores and restaurants was exempt from the requirement to obtain the rights holder's permission and pay a royalty fee under what was known as the 'business exemption' category. In order to qualify for this exemption, the size of the premises in which the music was played was limited to a certain area, by square footage.

The US claimed that this limitation on copyright protection fell within the TRIPS special case exemption, which captures the normal exploitation of the work and does not prejudice the legitimate interests of the rights holder. The WTO court didn't buy it. Ruling in favour of the complainant, Europe (presumably acting on behalf of European musicians and music-selling companies), the WTO panel disagreed with the US assertion. It noted that the size specified under the US exemption was quite large, meaning that a substantial majority of premises were covered by it, including those that would have the resources to pay royalty fees to the rights holders of the music. The US law was simply not protective enough of music rights holders.

The second major category of intellectual property protection under TRIPS is trademark. Trademarks, otherwise known as brands, are signs which distinguish certain goods and services from those produced by other companies. They can be words or logos or both. Even sounds can be trademarked, like the Apple computer start-up chime. Unlike copyright, which does not require formal registration, but simply exists as a matter of law whenever something original is created, trademarks must be registered with the government in order for them to be legally protected so that they cannot be reproduced without authorization. Trademarks can be among the most valuable assets of large multinationals, like the McDonald's golden arches and Apple's apple with a bite out of it, and product names like Coke or service names like Google. TRIPS defines what types of signs must be eligible for protection in all WTO member states and what the minimum rights conferred on their owners must be. The agreement also explains that member countries of the WTO are allowed to make registrability of trademarks dependent on the distinctiveness of the sign as acquired through use over time. Members are required to publish each trademark either before or immediately after it has been registered. This helps other businesses know that the owner intends to assert its rights over the sign, preventing accidental infringements.

Under TRIPS, trademarks that have been registered in any WTO member country grant the owner the exclusive right in all other member countries to prevent third parties from using the trademark without the owner's consent. This restriction applies to commercial uses of trademarks which are identical or similar for goods or services which are identical or similar to those for which the trademark was registered. The purpose of this guarantee is to prevent confusion among consumers in the marketplace, a situation which tends to be presumed when there is a sufficient degree of similarity. How precisely the notion of similarity will be determined is up to the domestic legal system of each member state. Unlike copyright, once registered, trademarks can be protected for an unlimited period. This reflects the essential commercial purpose of the trademark as distinct from copyrighted works of art, which have cultural value independent of their economic worth. Members may require that trademark registrations be renewed, but this may not be more than once every seven years. Members are free to determine any conditions attached to the licensing and assigning of trademarks under their national laws, although TRIPS maintains a prohibition on compulsory licensing of trademarks. Compulsory licensing, which we will return to shortly, is where the owner of the intellectual property is forced by law to allow a third party to use it subject to payment.

Geographical indications are another important category of intellectual property that is recognized by the TRIPS Agreement. Place names are often used to identify a product, and in so doing convey a certain degree of quality or unique characteristics that might be desirable to consumers. In that sense, geographical indications are rather like trademarks, except that they are always related to a particular geographical point of origin. So, for example, champagne is a variety of sparkling white wine that comes from the Champagne region of France and nowhere else, although you will likely hear people use that word to describe similar products coming from other places. Likewise, Scotch is a variety of whisky that originates in Scotland and only Scotland, even if some might say they are drinking Scotch when it's actually Irish or even American whiskey. A few years ago, Cornish pasties were granted geographical indication status by the EU, meaning that only pasties (a type of golden-brown pastry usually filled with meat and vegetables) made in Cornwall according to the traditional recipe are legally allowed to be sold as Cornish pasties. These products can be contrasted with sardines, which, as we saw earlier, are a generic type of fish that can be found all over the world, irrespective of the fact that the word 'sardine' was originally associated with Sardinia and the Mediterranean Sea.

A condition of TRIPS is that WTO members must make sure that they prevent the misuse of place names by competitors seeking to take unfair advantage of the goodwill associated with products from particular locations and thus misleading consumers. TRIPS clarifies that in order to qualify for geographical indication status under any member's national laws, it is not necessary to show that the product from that geographical area is in fact better or different from a similar product that comes from somewhere else. All that must be shown is that a particular reputation or goodwill has been established in that location with respect to that product, meaning that consumers are choosing to buy that particular variety of good because of its association with that place and its distinctive tradition or culture. To avoid the use of a geographical indicator that misleads the public in this respect, producers may use qualifying words like 'imitation' or 'like', such as 'Basmati-style' rice or 'Roquefort-style' cheese.

The makers of alcoholic beverages tend to be quite concerned about geographical indications because this is a vital component of their distinctiveness and therefore their competitive advantage. Recognizing this, TRIPS grants higher levels of protection for geographical indicators for wines and spirits. Competitors may not use the geographical name to link with their product even where there is no danger of the public being misled, and there is no provision to qualify the product's origin using 'imitation; or 'like' as I mentioned above. So, for example, sparkling wine from Chile could not be labelled 'sparkling wine in the style of champagne, made in Chile'. A special additional agreement on geographical indications for wines is being negotiated as part of the Doha Round agenda. This is a source of some disagreement among WTO members. The extra protection for wines and spirits is viewed by some as a legitimate way of protecting hard-won reputational advantages, whereas others see the tougher rules as an unnecessary restriction on marketing that is ultimately against consumer interests. People take their drinks seriously.

Some exceptions for protected geographical indication status are allowed under TRIPS, such as if the name has already become a generic term and it is now too late to restrict the association to a particular location. For example, cheddar now refers to a particular type of medium-hard yellowish cheese but it does not have to come from Cheddar, England, where it was originally made centuries ago. Parmesan cheese, as it is now known in most English-speaking countries outside of Europe (originally Parmigiano-Reggiano cheese from Italy), also falls within this exception.

Probably the most economically important as well as controversial category of intellectual property protection under the TRIPS Agreement is patents. TRIPS establishes that patent protection must be made available under the national laws of member states for both products and processes in almost all fields of technology. Minimum rights for patent holders are outlined in the TRIPS. Patent protection must be made available for inventions for at least twenty years, meaning that, after the elapse of this time, the underlying inventions may be reproduced lawfully without any payment or royalties or permission from the original patent holder. The twenty-year minimum time frame is intended to balance the incentives needed to encourage innovation and creativity, while ensuring that useful inventions may be widely disseminated to maximize their value to society, once the original inventor has been sufficiently rewarded for their work. TRIPS requires that patents must confer exclusive rights on the patent holder to sell the relevant product or process and to assign or license it to third parties.

Patents must be available under the national laws of member states for both products and processes and are extended in almost all fields of technology. Governments may refuse to issue a patent if its commercial exploitation is disallowed for reasons of public order or morality. It is also acceptable under TRIPS for governments to decline to register patents for plants and animals or for surgical or diagnostic methods. The rationale for these latter exceptions is that it is in the public interest to have useful medical procedures made as widely available as possible.

One key section of TRIPS reiterates the principles that were seen in the General Exceptions of the GATS and GATT which we looked at in chapter 5. Members are free to exclude from patentability inventions which deserve to be protected from commercial exploitation because they are necessary to serve various designated social goals. These are those which safeguard public order and public morality, or which protect human, animal or plant life or health, or which serve an environmental purpose. With clauses like this it is difficult to assert that the WTO is not tuned into things other than commerce and international trade. Clearly these exceptions must not be abused – if the member country is quite happy to allow the commercial exploitation of an invention that was created by one of its own nationals but attempts to restrict its patentability by a foreigner, then it will not be able to take advantage of this provision. It is about the way the law is applied, not the content of the law itself.

COMPULSORY LICENSING

Many millions of people in developing countries suffer and die every year from diseases like malaria and AIDS because they lack adequate medication. While there has been some success in dealing with AIDS in recent years, more than half of the world's population is still at risk of malaria. Many of the drugs that can treat these infectious diseases are readily available to affluent people in the West, where they are manufactured by pharmaceutical companies, often at considerable profit. Such products are protected by patent laws, which in one sense is only right given that these companies spent many millions of dollars in research and development in order to create them. On the other hand, the people who tend to need them the most, namely poor people in developing countries where malaria and AIDS have reached epidemic proportions, simply cannot purchase them on market terms like customers in Europe and North America can. In light of this dilemma, the TRIPS Agreement recognizes that sometimes patent holders can abuse their rights by failing to supply their inventions to the market at a price that is accessible to the people who need them. The TRIPS accordingly authorizes 'compulsory licensing', which allows competitors to copy the patented product under licence, provided that they make some reasonable financial contribution to the patent holder. Compulsory licensing is not granted lightly. There has to be a serious emergency or public health crisis, such as one caused by an epidemic, and the generic reproductions of patented medicines must only be for supply in the domestic market. Unfortunately, even with compulsory licensing, most of the countries that would need to use the compulsory licensing provision in order to combat the spread of deadly diseases like AIDS and malaria are the very ones that lack the technological ability to duplicate pharmaceuticals cheaply. In order to deal with this problem, the WTO decided in 2001 to allow generic copies of drugs made under compulsory licences to be exported to specific countries that lack production capacity. This means that developed countries are allowed under WTO law to manufacture generic medications on behalf of the listed poor countries that need them in emergency circumstances, and provided that some compensation is paid to the patent holder. Unfortunately 'emergency' and 'adequate compensation' are not defined under TRIPS. Many members, including Norway, Canada, India, the EU and now China have indicated their openness to such regimes as exporters of generic medicines to developing countries. Canada used the compulsory licensing scheme allowing the pharmaceutical company Apotex to export a generic AIDS medication to Rwanda. This provision of TRIPS, while controversial because it effectively takes property belonging to private companies, may be seen as an example of the WTO's attempts to rebalance the damaging inequality between the developed and developing world in relation to the vital issue of global health.

The patent provisions of TRIPS were called into question in 1997 in a dispute brought by Europe against India for its alleged failure to protect patents relating to pharmaceutical and agricultural chemical inventions. Europe was unhappy with India's largely informal regime for registering patents, which involved too much discretion on the part of administrative personnel to deny patents that had been registered through its 'mailbox patent' system. Mailbox patents was a procedure put in place for developing countries to fulfil their TRIPS obligations at lesser cost upon joining the WTO in 1995. It allowed them to have a system where patents could be registered initially through the mail, with the obligation to have a full patent registration system in place by 2005. The WTO panel ultimately ruled in favour of the EU, stating that India's interim system of mailbox patents was not sufficiently transparent and impartial – ordinary civil servants could deny the registration with little oversight. Worse, the panel ruled that India had failed to provide a mechanism for granting future patent holders the exclusive marketing rights that are mandated by TRIPS. The Indian government is still having difficulty agreeing on how to implement its patent laws in order to comply with this WTO ruling.

In addition to these substantive protections for particular forms of intellectual property, the TRIPS Agreement states that each member country must provide enforcement mechanisms for the protected rights through its own domestic legal system. These procedures must not be unnecessarily complicated or expensive, or else the rights enshrined in the agreement will be illusory. Judicial authorities must have the power to award cash compensation for infringements of intellectual property rights and to enforce criminal prosecution in situations of wilful piracy or counterfeiting on a commercial scale. Finally, the agreement clarifies that all of the TRIPS provisions themselves are enforceable under the WTO dispute settlement system. As with all the WTO agreements, this is essential for the obligations to take effect.

Non-Western concepts of intellectual property

One of the most widely cited problems with TRIPS is its alleged failure to recognize the intellectual property traditions of non-Western cultures, many of which are not formally recognized as legal rights. Medications developed by Indigenous tribes fall into this potentially enormous category of inventions which lack clear protection under national intellectual property laws and, by extension, the WTO and its TRIPS regime. Consequently, the commercial exploitation of these inventions without any compensation for those who discovered them has been provocatively termed 'bio-piracy'.

There are a number of commonly cited examples of bio-piracy, such as the use of rosy periwinkle, a plant found on the island of Madagascar and which had been used by Indigenous tribes for its medicinal properties possibly for centuries. The plant was later commercially reproduced by Western companies as a treatment for diabetes and various forms of cancer. The Mexican Enola bean was successfully patented under US law in the late 1990s, much to the consternation of Mexican farmers who had been growing it for generations. Thankfully that patent was ultimately revoked following a lawsuit brought on behalf of the farmers, allowing them to continue to cultivate it without having to pay any royalties. India has been a particularly vocal critic of the TRIPS Agreement because of its lack of coverage for traditional products (most notably seeds for use in agriculture) discovered by Indian Indigenous communities only for them to be subsequently patented by Western corporations.

While safeguarding the rights of Indigenous peoples is contemplated in international treaties like the 1992 Convention on Biological Diversity, which aims to ensure that lesser-developed countries can benefit from their resources and traditional knowledge, such provisions do not form part of TRIPS. This is viewed by many as a major gap in WTO policy and a source of continued tension between the developed and developing world; further discussion of this can be found in the next chapter.

This dilemma could possibly be addressed not so much by changing TRIPS itself but by encouraging Indigenous peoples, to take ownership of their traditional inventions in a manner that fits with the international understanding of intellectual property law and its established categories of copyright, trademark, patents, and so on. This strategy could ensure that Indigenous communities protect their entitlement to continue to use the things that have become part of their cultural heritage, often as a consequence of their own ingenuity, over centuries. Perhaps somewhat more ambitiously, this approach could also help them generate revenue, provided of course that the countries in which they live have the legal clout to prevent patent violations in foreign lands, which is unlikely given the cost of Western IP lawyers. This latter eventuality is particularly crucial given that numerous Indigenous groups around the world suffer from marginalization and low standards of living.

A fascinating example of how Indigenous peoples could take advantage of their cultural heritage can be seen in recent attempts to capture the goodwill associated with the Maasai tribal name. The Maasai tribe of Tanzania and Kenya has considered obtaining trademark protection for its name in order to sell things like clothes and sports apparel. It is believed that the public's association of the name Maasai with fierce and powerful warriors could be worth tens of millions of dollars as a marketing strategy for all sorts of products each year. Yet, currently, several companies use the brand Maasai (or variations of it) without any compensation to the tribe and its people, many of whom struggle with poverty. Part of the problem with the Maasai getting the protection of conventional IP laws like trademark is that some of these companies, like car manufacturer Land Rover, have already obtained trademark protection for the Maasai brand, necessitating courts revisiting the earlier granting of formal, recognizable legal protection. For the WTO's part, the TRIPS does not have any mechanism for ensuring that its member countries make efforts to assist Indigenous peoples in securing legal protection for their traditional inventions. While such requirements may be seen as laudable, they would likely be perceived as excessive interference by the WTO with each country's intellectual property laws as well as its relations with its own Indigenous communities.

Problems with conforming to TRIPS

Satisfying the requirements of the TRIPS Agreement was not a big deal for most developed countries, where intellectual property laws were a long-established feature of the legal system, and indeed a key component of a functioning economy. This is how the TRIPS was able to come into being along with the WTO itself in 1995 as one of the mandatory covered agreements like GATT and GATS. In recognition of the fact that it would be difficult for many non-industrialized countries to bring their laws into conformity with the requirements of TRIPS, the agreement provided for transitional or phase-in periods for developing countries, allowing them several additional years to do so. All of these have now expired, except for certain limited exceptions for the least developed countries (the very poorest ones) with respect to pharmaceutical patents, which were extended until 2016.

A number of newly industrializing countries had significant difficulties in complying with the WTO's intellectual property regime, largely due to a near total historic lack of appreciation for laws that safeguard artistic and technological creativity. The enforcement of intellectual property rights has been particularly difficult in China. One of the chief reasons for China's struggle in conforming to the TRIPS was the lack of awareness within

RUSSIAN IP LAWS

Russia languished for almost twenty years trying to become a member of the WTO before finally being accepted on board in 2012. One of the major stumbling blocks to Russia's accession, in addition to its long-standing tensions with neighbouring Ukraine, was its own inadequate intellectual property regime. Internet piracy in particular was rampant, with most Western movies and music easily available and shareable through websites like VKontakte (the Russian version of Facebook). The situation with ebooks was even worse, with some estimates that as much as ninety-two percent of ebooks downloaded in Russia was done so unlawfully. Because of ridiculously high prices to access foreign entertainment lawfully, resorting to pirated materials was the only option for many Russians, as my Russian students explained to me quite earnestly during our class on TRIPS. The problem had become so bad in the eyes of the West (especially the US) that it was only when Russia demonstrated a clear inclination to reform its intellectual property laws in the run-up to its formal accession that the rest of the WTO member- ship began to take the country seriously. Unlike some other recent entrants into the WTO family, the severity of the piracy epidemic in Russia led to the country not being granted a phase-in period for its TRIPS obligations. This meant that, as soon as it joined, the Russian government was immediately required to investigate and prosecute companies that illegally distributed copyrighted materials either over the Internet or physically. As a consequence of its efforts in this area, Russia was able to reduce significantly the quantity of coun- terfeit physical goods (mostly DVDs and CDs) and, more importantly, online piracy. In addition to complying with all of the TRIPS obli- gations calling for minimum protection of copyrights, trademarks, patents and other types of intellectual property, as a condition of membership to the WTO, Russia was also required to follow through with the TRIPS obligations to maintain intellectual property registra- tion and enforcement procedures, including criminal ones. Part of this involved the creation of an intellectual property-specific court within Russia's commercial court system. Created in 2013, the IPR (Intellectual Property Rights) Court was modelled on the specialized intellectual property courts of other jurisdictions, notably Germany. The new court is in Moscow and is composed of thirty judges who have expertise in both intellectual property law and technology. Of course, all of these positive changes can only mean more profits for the artists who create the movies and songs enjoyed by Russians, as well as more work for properly trained and likely expensive intellec- tual property lawyers who will want their own piece of the action.

China that copyright and trademark infringement is illegal. While China's modern intellectual property laws date from as far back as 1982, institutions for formal training in intellectual property law were not established until the late 1990s. Furthermore, as with many regulatory issues in China, there was significant tension between national, provincial and local authorities in the treatment of intellectual property rights. It has been pointed out by a number of commentators that some local governments in China did not wish to support anti-piracy and anti-counterfeit laws, creating obstacles for investigating authorities and in some cases hiding the illegal activities because of the revenue potential. It is difficult to eradicate lucrative crime where corruption is rife. One of the worst allegations in this regard has been that the Chinese government-owned search engine, Baidu, itself provides links to private websites that offer pirated services like movies and music, as well as access to counterfeit goods like luxury watches and handbags. This situation is somewhat paradoxical given that, last year, China reportedly issued more patents for inventions than the US for the first time in history.

India has been one of the major opponents of the WTO's intellectual property regime. Over the years India, which is an original member of the organization, has been able to modernize its intellectual property laws in order to conform to its WTO obligations. But a number of Western firms, notably US and Swiss pharmaceutical companies, still complain that India has been too quick to instigate compulsory licences for the reproduction of essential drugs when they should be using price controls to ensure affordability. For example, in 2012 India issued a compulsory licence for a kidney cancer drug made by the US company Bayer, selling it for less than one tenth of its price in the US. There is also concern that it is becoming increasingly difficult to obtain patent protection in India, with the number of granted and enforced patents falling abruptly in India over the past few years. Some have warned that this climate could result in TRIPS-based challenges through the WTO courts. As with other

WTO obligations, enforcement under TRIPS demands that the losing country must bring its IP laws into conformity with WTO obligations, in which case India would have to reform its patent laws to make it easier for firms to obtain such protection within its territory.

Brazil is one large emerging market WTO member that has responded remarkably well to its TRIPS obligations, establishing laws on copyright, trademarks and patents that correspond to those of most developed countries, although some believe that it still takes too long to register trademarks. There is also a specialized court to hear intellectual property claims. Whether the WTO is responsible for these improvements, which have been instrumental in attracting foreign investment and stimulating local innovation, is another debate. Many hold that the true reason for stronger intellectual property protection is that Brazilians now enjoy higher incomes as a consequence of overall improvements to their economy. People that once bought fake products can now afford the real thing.

Although the WTO's efforts to combat piracy and counterfeiting were initially aimed at satisfying the demands of powerful lobby groups in the US and other developed states, and indeed a number of developing countries resisted these efforts because of their potential to undercut the availability of Western products, the protection enshrined in the TRIPS Agreement is beginning to become globally accepted. In the future, firms from emerging markets, like India and China, that had once been suspicious of the WTO's intellectual property regime may come to rely on TRIPS-instigated intellectual property protection as they develop their own lucrative brands and inventions.

9
Trade is for everyone: the WTO and developing countries

Roughly two thirds of the 161 member countries of the WTO are classified as 'Developing', which is a commonly used euphemism for low-income, or as we used to say, 'Third World'. Because of their number and size in terms of population (over three quarters of the world's population), as well as their increasing importance in the global economy, developing countries are seen as a crucial focus of the WTO's efforts in regulating the smooth flow of goods and services around the world. International trade is now widely recognized as a vital ingredient of economic progress. In order for countries to make the transition from 'developing' to 'developed', they will increasingly rely on trade instead of handouts from wealthy countries in the form of aid, much of which is wasted. Indeed, the WTO encourages developed countries to focus their aid packages to the developing world to target improvements in their long-term capacity for trade – so-called Aid for Trade programmes.

This chapter will examine how the WTO regime has made special allowances for developing countries so that they enjoy the benefits of economic globalization without suffering as a consequence of their inability to withstand international competition, which is the obvious result of eliminating protectionism. I know I've been saying throughout this book that various issues are controversial, but in many ways this is the most pivotal debate surrounding the objectives and achievements of the WTO.

The WTO's treatment of developing countries is probably also the issue that has drawn the most criticism of the anti-globalizationists. These people tend, quite rightly in some cases, to criticize the WTO for its failure to liberalize trade in the goods which are of most practical use to the developing world in favour of pandering to the needs of the already wealthy West and its influential corporate lobby. This hypocrisy is perhaps best seen in the reality that the WTO (and GATT before it) has enabled an average tariff reduction from forty percent to four percent. But this applies only to 'industrialized goods', meaning goods that are manufactured or assembled, typically in large, automated factories. Such goods, like cars or refrigerators, tend not to be produced by developing countries, most of which are located in tropical or subtropical regions and which instead focus on agriculture and other raw commodities like coffee and sugar. Tariffs on many of these non-processed goods remain high, making it difficult for developing countries to compete on world markets. The problem is exacerbated because agricultural goods are heavily subsidized by Western governments; an issue which remains a serious sticking point in the Doha Round negotiations.

As I have attempted to show throughout this book, the WTO aims to enhance competition among producers by removing damaging distortions in the form of unnecessary, protectionist regulations. But, in reality, producers in many developing countries simply cannot withstand competition from foreign suppliers, which may have the advantage of superior technology and more highly trained workforces. The inability to cope with international competition for traded goods can be severely damaging – in some cases leading to mass unemployment, widespread poverty, or worse.

In considering the difficulties of developing country members, it must be made clear that the WTO is not a development agency.

It does not have as its central mission the advancement of peoples or governments in the developing world, although these things are expected to happen as a consequence of freer global trade. These activities do fall within the express mandate of other global institutions like the World Bank, or branches of the UN. While drawing attention to this misperception of the WTO's role might be an easy answer to the accusation that the WTO has failed in its job to help poor countries, the WTO does admit in its foundational treaty that 'there is need for positive efforts designed to ensure that developing countries, and especially the least developed among them, secure a share in the growth in international trade commensurate with the needs of their economic development'. In this sense, it is not incorrect to suggest that the economic development of poorer countries is one of the WTO's concerns, if indirectly so. Free trade on its own is insufficient if it only exacerbates inequalities and does not lead to raised standards of living and a growing volume of real income in all of the WTO's member states, not just the US, Europe, Canada, Australia and Japan. This is why the WTO has a number of rules that set out specifically to help poor countries.

Special and differential treatment

The WTO itself does not define 'developed' and 'developing' countries. This means that members announce for themselves whether they wish to be considered developed, developing or least developed countries when they join the WTO. The self-selection process itself continues to attract criticism, especially in relation to the large emerging markets like China and India, which have vast gross domestic products and major influence as world powers in terms of their capacity to negotiate trade concessions and to effect changes in the global economy. Why should these countries get special treatment when they have

enough money for space programmes, for example? This seeming hypocrisy is why other members can challenge the decision
of a member to take advantage of the various benefits available to
developing countries.

Generally speaking, most international organizations like the
UN, the World Bank and the IMF consider a developing country
to be one with a low level of industrialization (and consequently
an economic focus on agriculture), low income per person and
a deficient infrastructure. The status of 'developing' is also associated with lower standards of living in terms of health and length
of life as well as low levels of literacy and high infant mortal-
ity rates. Least developed countries tend to suffer these conditions most severely, and are often categorized by having a gross
national product per capita (the total amount of money earned
in that country divided by its population) of less than US $1000.
Accordingly, least developed countries get even more advantages
under the WTO regime than ordinary developing ones.

Most of the WTO rules aimed at assisting developing and least
developed countries can be found in the GATT, the WTO's chief
agreement covering international trade in goods. The GATT
contains a number of provisions that grant developing countries
exemptions from their commitments to remove protectionist
barriers to trade. This allows them to promote specific domestic
industries that are too weak to withstand foreign imports. The
key principle of GATT benefiting the WTO's lower-income
members is what's known as 'special and differential treatment'.
This encourages (but does not force) developed countries to grant
tariff concessions to developing countries on a non-reciprocal
basis – they give concessions in favour of exports from these
countries without the expectation of anything in return, which is
contrary to the WTO's main premise of negotiation. These provisions are primarily designed to increase developing countries'
trading opportunities through greater market access to other
countries.

Other WTO rules offer greater leniency to developing countries. For example, the prohibition on export-oriented subsidies that we looked at in chapter 4 does not apply to least developing countries under the Subsidies and Countervailing Measures agreement. Furthermore, the standards of proof required to substantiate a claim of subsidization brought against a developing country are more onerous, avoiding costly harassment of the governments of developing countries. Certain subsidies which would normally be actionable are not regarded as so when they are granted by developing country members in the context of privatization programmes where there has been debt forgiveness of the commercial enterprise.

The TRIPS Agreement discussed in the previous chapter has several substantive protections for developing countries, including the compulsory licensing provision. Under the Anti-Dumping Agreement, which we also explored in chapter 4, developed country members are instructed to take special care in exploring constructive remedies instead of imposing anti-dumping duties on developing countries. A WTO dispute settlement panel determined that this provision essentially means that developed countries should try to consider imposing a lesser duty than would be necessary to offset fully the margin of the dumped product.

Among the most important procedural advantages accorded to developing countries are the longer time frames to fulfil their obligations, which can be found in a number of WTO agreements. For example, under TRIPS, developing countries are entitled to a one-year delay in implementing the agreement, and a further five-year delay applies where a particular area of technology is currently not protectable under the domestic law of the particular developing country. Least developed countries were exempt from TRIPS obligations entirely for ten years, up until 2016. There are longer phase-in periods for developing countries to comply with health and safety regulations imposed by other members under the SPS and TBT agreements, which we considered in chapter 7.

Developing countries get additional time to respond to any complaints brought against them through the WTO dispute settlement procedure, as well as longer time frames to comply with rulings of the WTO court. As we saw in chapter 3, there is a very tight procedure associated with bringing or defending claims through the WTO dispute settlement system. Perhaps most significantly, developed country members of the WTO are required to exercise 'due restraint' in initiating trade disputes and claims for compensation against poorer countries. This policy is aimed at reducing the severity of the impact of some of the harsh consequences of the WTO rules that we have looked at throughout this book.

Generalized System of Preferences

The most significant measures in the GATT undertaken to assist developing countries are in the form of 'waivers', which means that developed country WTO members give up certain rights in relation to their dealings with developing ones. The first waiver is an exception to the most favoured nation guarantee of the GATT (which, as you will recall from chapter 2, requires all WTO members to treat goods originating from all other members the same under their domestic laws). This allows developed countries to grant preferential tariff treatment to developing countries through historic, largely colonial-based Generalized System of Preference schemes (or GSPs).

The second waiver also derogates from the most favoured nation principle by permitting developing countries to exchange these preferences among themselves. This means that one developing country can treat another developing country better than a third country if it wants to. The WTO encourages developing countries to get ahead by helping their friends in a similar position. Several Latin American countries do this under MERCOSUR (the Southern Common Market) and ASEAN (the Association of Southeast Asian Nations). These arrangements are important because some of the highest tariffs imposed on exports from low-income countries are those that are imposed by other low-income countries. Sometimes a developing country's worst enemy is another developing country.

GATT now further provides that, in the course of WTO trade negotiations, developing countries should not be required to make concessions that are inconsistent with their developmental, financial and trade needs. Rich countries are urged not to put pressure on a poorer one to do something it isn't ready for. This clause is tempered by what is known as the 'Graduation Clause'. The Graduation Clause states that as developing countries' capacity to make contributions or trade concessions increases along with their economic development, they are expected to participate more fully in the framework of rights and obligations under the GATT. A kind of 'take on more responsibility as you grow up' mentality. Unfortunately, precisely how the obligation to do more over time should be fulfilled is not specified. One of the key, often criticized, features of WTO's special treatment for developing countries is that the benefits extended by developed countries are voluntary and are meant to be temporary. So they can be withdrawn at any time, possibly even without notice. This can make it difficult for poorer countries to plan ahead.

Preferences extended by rich countries to poor ones through GSPs can be additionally problematic because they often have strings attached. The US and the EU GSPs in particular tend to impose a wide range of conditions on beneficiary countries, often relating to specific, sensitive goods like cotton (which has traditionally enjoyed subsidies within the US in part due to influential lobbies). GSPs are also often subject to conditions that are unrelated to trade, such as the beneficiary country's efforts to assist in attempts to combat terrorism or drug crime. Requirements that beneficiary countries conform to minimum standards of environmental or labour protection might be better received by the international community than those relating to terrorism, but they equally demonstrate the power imbalance between the rich country and the poor one. The legality of these types of non-trade conditions was confirmed by the WTO courts in a dispute brought by India against the EU. The EU had granted India some preferential trade concessions but only on condition that India cooperated in the prevention of drug trafficking.

In addition to ruling that this condition placed on a GSP was legal, the WTO Appellate Body further established in the EU–India dispute that trade preferences could be extended in a discriminatory fashion, meaning they could be granted to some developing country members and not other ones, even though this appeared to violate the GATT's most favoured nation principle. However, the Appellate Body clarified that trade preferences extended under GSPs had to be offered to all developing countries that were similarly situated in terms of their financial and economic needs. In other words, they had to be offered to all countries at the same level of development. The assessment of these needs by the developed country donor must be based on objective and transparent criteria. The one-size-fits-all idea of a developing country appears to have been thrown out of the window with this decision. The capacity for developed countries to dictate who can benefit from their GSPs is an important counterpoint to the recipient country's ability to designate itself as developing upon joining the WTO in the first place.

Developed country members of the WTO now clearly have significant room to decide which countries they will extend preferential treatment to in their GSPs. They can select criteria that they know only specific countries will be able to meet, provided of course that they can show that these criteria are objective and are based on developmental, financial and trade needs. This approach, while somewhat confusing in its lack of clarity, is obviously sensible. Without some freedom to control the terms of preferential trade arrangements with developing countries, it would have been very difficult for developed countries to impose any conditions on these schemes. This could have led to rich countries reducing or abandoning their preferential trading arrangements altogether. Better to have GSPs with strings attached than none at all.

This EU–India decision by the WTO's Appellate Body was condemned by a number of developing countries for entrenching artificial categories of developmental status among poor country members of the WTO, meaning that some countries might end up benefiting from preferential arrangements when they don't really need them. On the other hand, this ruling has been welcomed because it was recognized the political and economic reality of the wide range of developing countries, some of which are much more prosperous than others. The effect of developmental status is now more effectively controlled by donor countries, rather than by the beneficiary countries themselves, which may have a vested interest in depicting themselves as needy. In addition to large emerging markets like China, India and Brazil questionably enjoying the advantages of special and differential treatment, small, wealthy states like Hong Kong, South Korea and Taiwan continue to benefit under some old GSPs.

In order to qualify for the reduced tariffs available under GSPs, exported products must fulfil requirements relating to the identification of where they originate. Rules of origin of traded goods are therefore a key component of all GSPs. Clear notification of origin counters the potential for abuse of the preferential scheme by preventing a product from being exported from a country outside the scheme to a country within the scheme before being re-exported to the donor country. Rules of origin normally require that there is a minimum level of value added in the beneficiary country. Of course, the complexity of these rules tends to increase the more components there are in a given product, so in practice the more difficult rules are usually associated with highly manufactured goods rather than agricultural products. Complying with these rules may on its own impose a significant financial burden on some developing countries.

It should be noted that there are actually very few mandatory provisions in the WTO regime meant to increase, or at least equalize, the trading opportunities of developing countries. They tend to be optional, at the discretion of the developed country extending a GSP. As beneficiaries of the looser rules and MFN exceptions, developing countries are not in a position to make formal claims regarding their lack of increased trading opportunities. This problem is worsened by the fact that WTO courts have been unwilling to develop clear tests for interpreting and applying the special and differential treatment provisions found in the various WTO texts.

ECONOMIC PARTNERSHIP AGREEMENTS

There have been a number of criticisms of the historic GSP arrangements between rich countries and their former colonies. The benefits of the GSPs were generally concentrated on the more advanced developing countries that actually needed them the least, like India and the Philippines. Moreover, by the time the GSP provisions of the GATT were enacted in the 1970s, the difference between the preferential tariff rates under these agreements and normal tariff rates extended to all WTO members had already decreased substantially. This is one of the main reasons that trade arrangements with developing countries that contain more equal terms of trade are now being negotiated. These agreements, which are framed more as mutually beneficial treaties between equals rather than benevolent gifts, are known as Economic Partnership Agreements or EPAs. The modern EPAs implemented by the EU, the US and other developed countries are built around conventional WTO principles of reciprocity and non-discrimination. This means that the advantages extended by developed countries come at the expense of the developing partner granting access to its domestic market on the same terms, which is then extended to all developing states on a most favoured nation basis. As trade openness is potentially harmful to economically weaker countries, EPAs extend a gradual removal of all of the preferences which had been established under older GSPs. Longer phase-out periods apply to the most sensitive 'traditional' goods such as bananas, rum, rice and sugar. The reciprocal nature of EPAs, which still claim to have a development agenda, has led to significant criticisms from developing states which feel that they are not yet ready to absorb imports from developed countries on equal terms. EPAs must conform to the WTO's requirements for normal preferential trade agreements. Compliance of the EPAs with WTO rules on regional trade agreements rests upon the interpretation of the highly ambiguous concepts of 'on the whole' and 'substantially all trade' as discussed in chapter 2. As the old GSPs are recast as EPAs, these regimes will be removed from the scrutiny of the WTO entirely (other than the WTO's rules on normal preferential trading agreements), and the conformity of trading partners with the terms of these agreements will be adjudicated by agreement-specific arbitration panels, not the WTO courts.

Technical assistance and financial support

It is worth mentioning that there are a number of other, more mundane ways in which the WTO gives extra attention to developing countries. Chief among these is help in understanding and complying with WTO rules. As you can probably tell from reading this book, WTO rules can be complicated. This is why the WTO offers training and technical assistance to developing countries that request it relating to understanding and implementing WTO obligations. This assistance is called for in specific agreements such as the SPS and TBT, which are highly technical and consequently require much more regulatory oversight than is commonly available in countries with lower incomes. Technical training is offered through the WTO Secretariat in Geneva, essentially the executive branch of the organization. The Secretariat also has special legal advisers that can help out developing countries when they are engaged in a dispute in the WTO courts.

The WTO holds regular training sessions on trade policy in Geneva and organizes several hundred technical cooperation meetings annually, including various seminars and workshops of interest to trade representatives, trade lawyers and diplomats from developing countries. The WTO also engages in an integrated programme with other major international organizations like the IMF and the World Bank for a joint technical assistance programme exclusively for least developed countries.

In addition to these training services, which are used regularly, developing countries may take advantage of the Advisory Centre on WTO Law, which was established by thirty-two member countries in 2001 to help contribute to the cost of litigating using the WTO dispute settlement system. The Advisory Centre on WTO Law is an intergovernmental organization that is completely separate from the WTO itself. It has provided support in almost forty disputes since it was created, and all least developed countries are eligible to receive advice and assistance from it at no cost. Several WTO members on their own offer additional financial support for ministers and accompanying officials from least developed countries so that they can attend the high-level ministerial conferences which take place around the world.

Additionally, in 2002, the WTO adopted a faster membership process for least developed countries seeking to join the WTO. This should offer some comfort given the expense of complex accession negotiations, which can sometimes take several years or even decades.

Finally, as the WTO is headquartered in Geneva, this requires member states to send delegates there frequently, either as part of negotiations or committee membership, or if they are involved in a dispute. As anyone who has been to Switzerland knows, while the country's mountains and historic towns are beautiful (not to mention the chocolate and cheese), it is incredibly expensive. If hotels and restaurants are steep for tourists, you can imagine that maintaining office space in Geneva can be prohibitive for countries with low incomes. This is why only about one third of the thirty least developed countries in the WTO are able to do so. In order to resolve this difficulty, and to make participation in the WTO more feasible for the poorest countries, the Swiss government has generously agreed to provide subsidized office space for delegations from least developed countries. These premises can also help least developed countries take part in United Nations activities that take place in the UN's Geneva location across the street from the WTO.

THE BALI PACKAGE

As we explored in chapter 1, the ongoing Doha Development Round of trade negotiations, which began in 2001, has failed so far to achieve a number of important goals that are of interest to the WTO's poorer members. Some of the key issues still being negotiated include reforms to trade in agriculture, especially reductions in subsidization from the developed world, and the phasing out of quotas on exports of textiles and clothing. In December 2013, despite struggling with Doha, some progress was finally made in WTO negotiations in Bali, Indonesia. An agreement known as the Bali Package was reached between all WTO members, and it includes provisions for lowering import tariffs and agricultural subsidies. This issue was particularly thorny because of demands made by India that it should be allowed to maintain its domestic agricultural subsidies indefinitely in order to ensure security of the food supply, an issue that was of particular political relevance domestically due to upcoming Indian elections. Ultimately India was permitted to keep its agricultural subsidies for the time being, with the matter to be reconsidered within four years. Among the most important achievements of the Bali Package were the commitments made relating to trade facilitation, which we looked at briefly in chapter 2. Trade facilitation refers to attempts to streamline bureaucratic problems associated with goods crossing borders, like unnecessary customs duties and inspections, as well as bribery and corruption. These things can extend border crossings in some least developed countries by days or even weeks, often leading to the spoliation of perishable goods. Studies showed that inefficient procedures can raise the cost of traded goods by up to fifty percent, a figure that is often higher when the goods are shipped by women, who regularly suffer harassment or are forced to pay higher bribes. Modernization of these practices with the help of technology as well as the simple removal of red tape should shorten some critical border crossings down to a few hours, similar to what they would be in the developed world. As a result of earlier WTO efforts in trade facilitation, several African countries were able to establish one-stop border crossings involving closer cooperation between the border agencies, including the Chirundu crossing between Zambia and Zimbabwe and the Malaba crossing between Kenya and Uganda.

As with many aspects of the WTO regime, the organization's treatment of developing countries is controversial, perhaps exceptionally so. Critics complain that the special and differential treatment provisions are inadequate to address the very severe imbalances in economic power as well as geopolitical influence. It is often pointed out, in some respects quite rightly, that a level playing field is a misnomer when it comes to developing countries which cannot handle intense competition from foreign goods. Simply giving them the same opportunities as rich countries is not enough – they need distinct advantages to survive the trade game, but of course this is antithetical to the concept of non-discrimination, which is one of the cornerstones of liberalized trade and a foundational principle of the WTO itself.

Given the vast number of countries and people who fall within the category of developing, the WTO can no longer afford to sideline these concerns if it wants to maintain, or some would say obtain, credibility as a truly international organization aimed at bettering the lives of people worldwide rather than simply entrenching the advantages enjoyed by Western corporations and consumers. Nowhere are these complaints more acute than in the context of agricultural subsidies maintained by members like the US and Europe. Were these policies removed or even curtailed, it could translate to improvements in the lives of many hundreds of millions of people in Africa.

Still, the WTO has instigated a number of vital policies intended to ensure that the benefits of free trade are more widely shared across the global community. Non-reciprocal preferential arrangements like the GSPs and phased-in EPAs are vital instruments of economic growth and productivity for many developing member states. Less strict implementation of rules on trade tools like subsidies and dumping as well as more generous time frames and a number of comprehensive training programmes have also gone a long way to soften some of the burdens associated with the world trading system. These techniques are far from perfect, but continued negotiations for further concessions for developing countries still under way at the WTO during Doha and possibly beyond are encouraging.

Conclusion: the future of the WTO

As dawn broke over the Swiss Alps on the first day of 2015, a monumental moment in the economic history of the world took place. The World Trade Organization, once nothing more than a twinkle in the eye of the Bretton Woods visionaries, turned twenty. While I suspect that there were probably a few handshakes and certainly some congratulations within the halls of the Centre William Rappard, possibly even a cake with or without candles, there was undoubtedly very little in the way of celebrations across the globe, either in the capital cities of the WTO's vast 'empire' or in the boardrooms of the world's great companies.

The WTO is no longer a teenager, and perhaps it should no longer be seen as one. While observers have always taken the WTO seriously, because of its impact on international trade and by extension on the global economy, we have remained somewhat less confident about its capacity to govern itself, to act without the influence of its most powerful members – the US, the EU and the generation of Western trade diplomats that first conceived of the GATT and the Bretton Woods system as the antidote to a war-ravaged, depression-scarred world. The WTO can never exist apart from the will of its members, we know that. This is what you get by being a democratic organization, even if the voting process isn't quite perfect. We also know that it is meaningless to say, even as it has matured in its role as an international organization, that the WTO has any true purpose outside its mission to capture the benefits of comparative advantage.

But it may be time, in the light of its many successes in achieving greater commitments to trade liberalization and resolving potentially damaging international disputes, to let the WTO work things through on its own without the interference of the machinations of its members' many quarrelsome and defiant politicians. Fully released from the tentacles of their posturing masters at home, trade representatives to the WTO could begin to see themselves as parts of a larger organization rather than as extensions of their own governments. A truly international organization, rather than a collection of individuals, would be better placed to crystallize the vision of liberalized trade into reality. Some might counter that such a suggestion is an affront to the very sovereignty that peaceful economic relations are meant to serve. One thing is certain – the WTO will continue to struggle to make further progress while its members remain uncommitted to the ideal of free trade.

The dilemma of the WTO's reliance on the will of its members is in one sense an embodiment of its greatest strength. I hope this book has shown how the WTO has tried and very often succeeded in staying locked in to its mission to increase the flow of international trade by minimizing legal barriers imposed by its member countries. Much of the WTO's ingenuity can be seen in its tireless capacity to defer to the wishes of its members, skilfully sidestepping some of the greatest controversies like health and the environment, through its unabashed focus on the prevention of discrimination and other market distortions in the guise of legitimate policy goals.

Clearly its goal of enhancing trade has inevitably caused the organization to drift into other policy areas, like the environment, labour and health, or more obviously economic ones like member countries' efforts to safeguard their own economies from the damaging effects of recession. Its failure to address some of the negative consequences of globalization has made the WTO the target of critics who argue that the organization must be more humane, or that it needs to enlarge its mandate to cover the social issues that matter to real people, rather than concentrating on the bottom line of trading multinationals. I'm not convinced that diluting the WTO's role to cover such issues would help it liberalize trade, nor would it enable it to deal with these other policy issues in a way that would be useful to the world's citizens. These matters are rightly the sphere of national elected governments. In my view, the WTO already has enough on its plate in delivering deeper trade liberalization without it becoming some kind of world court on all sorts of social issues, as important as they are.

It seems to me that the WTO has done a good job in staying the course when it has been faced with all sorts of other regulatory issues. It has done so in a manner that has been mindful of the need to enhance global trade flows to advantage all people, not just those in the richest countries, even if this goal has not been fully realized yet. The will of the international community to raise the living standards of the world's poorest people through trade appears to be there, even if it hasn't worked perfectly. Progress in this sphere can only be achieved with the cooperation of the world's most powerful countries, many of which continue to impose trade-distorting subsidies on things like agricultural produce. Multilateral consensus on these matters will be difficult.

We must not ignore (nor should we exaggerate) the role that the WTO has played in the rise of the emerging markets, the increasing dominance of which has become perhaps the most monumental change of the twenty-first century so far. To the extent that this is the consequence of the success of the neo-liberal model of economic relations of which the WTO is emblematic, it is a phenomenon that must be celebrated with caution. Just as the reduction of barriers to trade in goods and services has opened up the markets of countries like China, India and Brazil, unlocking low-cost industrialization on a massive scale, liberalized international trade has also perpetrated a less pleasing side effect in the West. It is undeniable that hundreds of millions of people have been brought out of poverty in Asia, Africa and

Latin America because of globalization, which has both brought employment and made once unimaginable things affordable. But at the same time, this force has also conspired to destroy manufacturing jobs in North America and Europe, lucrative work that many of your parents (and mine) did for years, allowing them to buy homes, take holidays and have families.

As every angst-conscious politician seems to be telling us now, our societies in the West are becoming more unequal – with wealth concentrating increasingly into the hands of fewer and fewer individuals. While some might see this as a rousing call to justice, to others the politics of envy is a startlingly effective strategy. Rising inequality in the West has been the target of many riots and protests, like the controversial Occupy movement of 2011. This tension is also played out intergenerationally. Post-war baby boomers retire into multiple-home luxury with pensions indexed to inflation while the youth of today struggle simply to pay off their student loans and escape their parents' basements to rent dingy apartments. There's not much chance that they will get into secure jobs and onto the much-vaunted 'property ladder' like their parents did, at least not until the baby boomers die off.

This disparity has translated not only into social upheavals, but a widespread disdain for capitalism's work/wage bargain. Having a good job and getting ahead now appears to be synonymous with greed and exploitation. Hollywood, ever the barometer of mass consciousness, churns out one movie after the other with this theme, *The Wolf of Wall Street* being perhaps the most celebrated recent offering. Even Pope Francis has climbed aboard the anti-capitalist bandwagon, declaring that the idolatry of money and the belief in the absolute power of the market are among the chief ills of our time. After the crisis of 2008–09 and the high-profile bailouts of banks on both sides of the Atlantic, the financial sector seems to remain the favoured target, with many forgetting that some Western economies, like the UK, depend heavily on this sector to stay afloat. Many others who recognize this dependency lament it.

Are the lost generation of Western youth and the disappearance of the comfortable blue-collar lifestyle welcome trade-offs for the demise of poverty in the developing world? Should we be happy that the middle classes of North America and Europe are being hollowed out so that farmers in China can buy their first home and send their children to university? Is it a cause for celebration that worldwide inequality has shrunk for the first time since the Industrial Revolution, even as millennials come to terms with the fact that they won't do as well as their parents?

As the handmaiden of globalization, the WTO is at least partially answerable for these trends. Whether or not other things, like technology, should also be 'blamed' for declining wages in the West and the rise of the Chinese middle class is a matter for economists to resolve, but of course no one would suggest that we 'turn off' the Internet, even if we could. Some studies have shown that the WTO has played an almost negligible role in the economic advancement of its members. This is perhaps most troubling to me as I try to get students to take my course every year. Thankfully other studies reveal a strong correlation between WTO accession and the rise of GDP, particularly for countries that were already industrialized or well on their way.

Even if its role in the rebalancing of the global economy at the expense of some national ones were taken as established, it is far from certain that the WTO as an organization can give us any meaningful guidance as to which people deserve to get ahead through its brand of globalization, or whether any progress achieved at the expense of someone else's downfall is justified. These are moral judgments, probably best left for philosophers, not economists, and certainly not lawyers, at least not those who teach WTO law.

What is perhaps more obvious is that for the WTO to quit now, for the world to turn its back on trade liberalization and to allow protectionism to reign (again), would almost certainly be a disaster. If the relentless forward pace of globalization means that nothing stays the same, it may also be true, as someone once said (or sang), that some things will be coming around again. Chinese wages are rising by close to twenty percent per year, while those in the West have fallen. This makes manufacturing in China already much less profitable than it was only a few years ago. The new phenomenon of 're-shoring' – the relocation of factories and call centres back to developed countries – has begun to pick up pace. The extraction of shale gas may soon make energy and with it heavy industry cheaper in the US and Europe than it has been for decades. This means that exports of manufactured goods from the developed world may soon compete with those from Asia. We may be witnessing the rebirth of American and European industry, but not as a consequence of trade barriers imposed by politicians bent on satisfying the pro-union lobby, but because of the very forces of globalization that killed manufacturing to begin with.

What now appear to be natural cyclical processes cannot happen without the benefit of anti-protectionist rules at the international level. Whether these come from the WTO or from regional trade agreements like the Transatlantic Trade and Investment Partnership and the Trans-Pacific Partnership remains to be seen. As the global economy balances out and the distinction between rich and poor countries blurs, the WTO's continued relevance is uncertain. It may be that deeper economic linkages involving things like investment, competition and monetary policy will require a shift of focus to the bilateral arena where negotiations are easier. Or there may be an enlargement of the WTO's current mandate, capturing not just social issues, but transforming it into a World Economic Organization rather than one with trade as its sole purpose. Or, the WTO could shrink, turning its attention away from multilateral negotiations of new disciplines to the resolution of disputes over existing commitments, more of a trade court than a negotiating forum. None of these scenarios would surprise me. Most institutions, whether they are companies, countries or sports teams, are like individuals; they need to reinvent themselves to stay relevant, just as the GATT was recast into the WTO some twenty years ago on a cold January day at the dawn of a new global era.

One thing is certain – globalization is here to stay. The old world of isolated island countries and independent economies is long gone and will not return, at least not any time soon. So, the task of international institutions like the WTO, which may one day replace national governments as the final arbiters of rules as well as power and influence, is to adapt to globalization's ups and downs and, above all else, remain responsive to the needs of all the world's citizens, whatever those needs might be.

Further reading

1 How it works: the structure and function of the WTO

Simon Lester, Bryan Mercurio and Arwel Davies, *World Trade Law: Text, Materials and Commentary*, 2nd edn (Oxford: Hart Publishing, 2012), chs 1 and 2.

Michael Trebilcock, *Advanced Introduction to International Trade Law* (Northampton, MA: Edward Elgar, 2015), ch. 1.

Michael Trebilcock, Rob Howse and Antonia Eliason, *The Regulation of International Trade*, 4th edn (Abingdon, Oxon: Routledge, 2013), ch. 1.

Peter Van den Bossche and Werner Zdouc, *The Law and Policy of the World Trade Organization*, 3rd edn (Cambridge: Cambridge University Press, 2013), chs. 1 and 2.

2 The three pillars: the principles of tariff reduction, non-discrimination and transparency

Lorand Bartels and Frederico Ortino (eds), *Regional Trade Agreements and the WTO Legal System* (Oxford: Oxford University Press, 2007).

Simon Lester, Bryan Mercurio and Arwel Davies, *World Trade Law: Text, Materials and Commentary*, 2nd edn (Oxford: Hart Publishing, 2012), chs 6, 7, 8.

Michael Trebilcock, *Advanced Introduction to International Trade Law* (Northampton, MA: Edward Elgar, 2015), chs 3, 4, 5.

Michael Trebilcock, Rob Howse and Antonia Eliason, *The Regulation of International Trade*, 4th edn (Abingdon, Oxon: Routledge, 2013), chs 2, 3, 4 and 7.

Peter Van den Bossche and Werner Zdouc, *The Law and Policy of the World Trade Organization*, 3rd edn (Cambridge: Cambridge University Press, 2013), chs 4, 5, 6.

3 In the courtroom: the WTO dispute settlement system

Michelle Grando, *Evidence, Proof, and Fact-Finding in WTO Dispute Settlement* (Oxford: Oxford University Press, 2010).

Simon Lester, Bryan Mercurio and Arwel Davies, *World Trade Law: Text, Materials and Commentary*, 2nd edn (Oxford: Hart Publishing, 2012), ch. 5.

Andrew Mitchell, *Legal Principles in WTO Disputes* (Cambridge: Cambridge University Press, 2008).

Michael Trebilcock, *Advanced Introduction to International Trade Law* (Northampton, MA: Edward Elgar, 2015), ch. 2.

Michael Trebilcock, Rob Howse and Antonia Eliason, *The Regulation of International Trade*, 4th edn (Abingdon, Oxon: Routledge, 2013), ch. 5.

Peter Van den Bossche and Werner Zdouc, *The Law and Policy of the World Trade Organization*, 3rd edn (Cambridge: Cambridge University Press, 2013), ch. 3.

4 Playing fair: non-tariff barriers to trade

Gary Horlick, *World Trade Organization and International Trade Law: Antidumping, Subsidies and Trade Agreements* (New Jersey: World Scientific, 2013).

Simon Lester, Bryan Mercurio and Arwel Davies, *World Trade Law: Text, Materials and Commentary*, 2nd edn (Oxford: Hart Publishing, 2012), chs 10 and 11.

Michael Trebilcock, *Advanced Introduction to International Trade Law* (Northampton, MA: Edward Elgar, 2015), chs 6 and 7.

Michael Trebilcock, Rob Howse and Antonia Eliason, *The Regulation of International Trade*, 4th edn (Abingdon, Oxon: Routledge, 2013), chs 9 and 10.

Peter Van den Bossche and Werner Zdouc, *The Law and Policy of the World Trade Organization*, 3rd edn (Cambridge: Cambridge University Press, 2013), chs 11 and 12.

5 Money isn't everything: public interest exceptions to WTO rules

Simon Lester, Bryan Mercurio and Arwel Davies, *World Trade Law: Text, Materials and Commentary*, 2nd edn (Oxford: Hart Publishing, 2012), ch. 9.

Krista Nadakavukaren Schefer, *Social Regulation in the WTO: Trade Policy and International Legal Development* (Northampton, MA: Edward Elgar, 2010).

Michael Trebilcock, *Advanced Introduction to International Trade Law* (Northampton, MA: Edward Elgar, 2015), chs 14 and 15.

Michael Trebilcock, Rob Howse and Antonia Eliason, *The Regulation of International Trade*, 4th edn (Abingdon, Oxon: Routledge, 2013), chs 17 and 18.

Peter Van den Bossche and Werner Zdouc, *The Law and Policy of the World Trade Organization*, 3rd edn (Cambridge: Cambridge University Press, 2013), ch. 8.

6 Not just things: the liberalization of trade in services

Panagiotis Delimatsis, *International Trade in Services and Domestic Regulations* (Oxford: Oxford University Press, 2007).

Nicolas Diebold, *Non-Discrimination in International Trade in Services* (Cambridge: Cambridge University Press, 2010).

Simon Lester, Bryan Mercurio and Arwel Davies, *World Trade Law: Text, Materials and Commentary*, 2nd edn (Oxford: Hart Publishing, 2012), ch. 14.

Michael Trebilcock, *Advanced Introduction to International Trade Law* (Northampton, MA: Edward Elgar, 2015), ch. 10.

Michael Trebilcock, Rob Howse and Antonia Eliason, *The Regulation of International Trade*, 4th edn (Abingdon, Oxon: Routledge, 2013), ch. 13.

7 Health and safety: food and product standards as barriers to trade

Tracy Epps, *International Trade and Health Protection: A Critical Assessment of the WTO's SPS Agreement* (Northampton, MA: Edward Elgar, 2008).

Simon Lester, Bryan Mercurio and Arwel Davies, *World Trade Law: Text, Materials and Commentary*, 2nd edn (Oxford: Hart Publishing, 2012), ch. 13.

Michael Trebilcock, *Advanced Introduction to International Trade Law* (Northampton, MA: Edward Elgar, 2015), ch. 13.

Michael Trebilcock, Rob Howse and Antonia Eliason, *The Regulation of International Trade*, 4th edn (Abingdon, Oxon: Routledge, 2013), ch. 8.

Peter Van den Bossche and Werner Zdouc, *The Law and Policy of the World Trade Organization*, 3rd edn (Cambridge: Cambridge University Press, 2013), chs 13 and 14.

8 Keeping it real: the protection of intellectual property rights

Carlos Correa (ed.), *Research Handbook on the Protection of Intellectual Property under WTO Rules* (Northampton, MA: Edward Elgar, 2012).

Simon Lester, Bryan Mercurio and Arwel Davies, *World Trade Law: Text, Materials and Commentary*, 2nd edn (Oxford: Hart Publishing, 2012), ch. 17.

Michael Trebilcock, *Advanced Introduction to International Trade Law* (Northampton, MA: Edward Elgar, 2015), ch. 12.

Michael Trebilcock, Rob Howse and Antonia Eliason, *The Regulation of International Trade*, 4th edn (Abingdon, Oxon: Routledge, 2013), ch. 14.

Peter Van den Bossche and Werner Zdouc, *The Law and Policy of the World Trade Organization*, 3rd edn (Cambridge: Cambridge University Press, 2013), ch. 15.

9 Trade is for everyone: the WTO and developing countries

Simon Lester, Bryan Mercurio and Arwel Davies, *World Trade Law: Text, Materials and Commentary*, 2nd edn (Oxford: Hart Publishing, 2012), ch. 18.

Sonia Rolland, *Development at the WTO* (Oxford: Oxford University Press, 2012).

Chantal Thomas and Joel Trachtman (eds), *Developing Countries in the WTO Legal System* (Oxford: Oxford University Press, 2009).

Michael Trebilcock, *Advanced Introduction to International Trade Law* (Northampton, MA: Edward Elgar, 2015), ch. 16.

Michael Trebilcock, Rob Howse and Antonia Eliason, *The Regulation of International Trade*, 4th edn (Abingdon, Oxon: Routledge, 2013), ch. 16.

Index